# ENTER, ENLIGHTEN, AND EXIT

A Simple Guide to Making
Clear, Concise, and Convincing
Presentations

Deborah Weissman Ostreicher

**Enter, Enlighten, and Exit**
Copyright © 2021 by Deborah Weissman Ostreicher

Published by PR Bulldog Press

For inquiries, please contact distinguishedcomm.com

ISBN 978-1-7376142-0-3 paperback
ISBN 978-1-7376142-1-0 ebook

Author photo courtesy of Tom Eglin
Photos in Chapter 3 courtesy of Lena Weissman
All other photos courtesy of Shutterstock

Many thanks go out to the book project team:
Kent Sorsky, editor
Davidson Belluso, cover designer
Carla Green, book designer

# Contents

Becoming a clear, concise and convincing presenter is *not* just a matter of "practice makes perfect." If you practice terrible habits over and over, you may become perfect at being terrible.

# Foreword

"Just be yourself." Three common words of encouragement that seem straightforward, yet upon further reflection don't really help most people as they approach the microphone.

As a public speaking professor, I consistently encounter students who believe that presentation abilities are something you are born with. They think that to be effective they must transform into some charismatic character who is completely different from themselves. In reality, people possess everything they need to captivate an audience; they must simply be shown how to do it.

I have witnessed countless individuals transform their speaking abilities using the tools in this book—even those with the worst anxieties and aversions to public speaking. The most magnificent part of this material is that it can be applied to any communication situation. Whether you are speaking one-on-one, to a roomful of people, in person, or online, this book contains the skills you need to leave a positive and lasting impression with your audience.

Having known the author for over two decades, I can personally attest to her expertise in the field of communication. It is hard to ignore her ability to deliver persuasive and memorable messages. Yet even more impressive is her willingness to teach and inspire others to do the same. She is an example to all educators, managers, and leaders of the magic that lies in focusing on the strengths someone already has, as opposed to pointing out what they lack.

Be forewarned that the skills you'll learn from this book will spill over into all facets of your life. When you gain the ability to take any type of material and formulate it in ways that your audience can connect with, you hold the power to form deeper connections with all people. This innovative and highly sought-after set of skills will help elevate your professional *and* your personal self, while allowing you to find enjoyment in presenting information to anyone at any time.

Congratulations on taking the first steps in learning how to Enter with a bang, Enlighten your audience, and Exit like a pro. May you finally understand what it truly means to "just be yourself."

—Mary Zatezalo, Professor of Communication,
Arizona State University

# Introduction

Few activities generate as much anxiety as the thought or act of giving a speech. Whether it's to a small group of peers or to a room of 500 strangers, presenters often face the same amount of fear and uncertainty.

What does it mean to be an "effective" presenter? Does it mean "good"? "Funny"? "Inspirational"? It might. But more importantly, is the presenter accomplishing what they set out to achieve? Is the audience getting the intended message? Are they responding to the speaker? If the answer is yes to all of those questions, then the speaker is effective.

So how can *you* be an effective presenter?

Here's the good news: **There's no set formula**.

Every individual and circumstance provides a unique opportunity to be effective.

Here's the bad news: **There's no set formula.**

Every presenter and situation is different, and it takes some work to find your individual approach.

More good news: If you follow the guidance in this book, you will be well on your way to becoming a better presenter.

> ## A presentation or speech should always be thought of as a *conversation*.

As a longtime communications director for large organizations, I was often asked to develop "canned" speeches on various topics so that anyone on the team could deliver them. Yet since I never wrote out scripts, and I changed my presentations depending on the audience, I found it was not possible to hand over "company standard" presentations—at least not *effective* ones.

Let's face it; people know when someone is reciting a canned speech or reading a script, and that is a recipe for disaster. Jeff can't effectively deliver Jen's presentation and Jen can't effectively deliver Jeff's. The best presentations will be unique to the presenter.

What I did instead to help my organization was to rely on the advice of excellent mentors, professional training, a lot of experience, and some help from Aristotle to develop a presentation system that works. Rather than provide my colleagues with a collection of canned speeches to deliver on every topic, I developed a system that would enable them to present in a way that best matched their individual personality and their audience.

For example, some people felt comfortable integrating a lot of impromptu audience interaction and questions throughout their presentations, while others liked a more controlled exchange. Once presenters found a style that worked for them, they just got better and better. During the course of over two decades with the City of Phoenix as an airport executive, communications director, and political staffer, and while training hundreds of students there, I refined my system, known as Enter, Enlighten, and Exit (EEE).

Based on this presentation system, I began Distinguished Communications to help speakers express themselves in an effective and impactful way. As I work with clients from different backgrounds and experience levels, my faith in the EEE system continues. I see terrified speakers become effective and confident presenters, and I see seasoned speakers polish their skills to reach new heights. The system works because it draws on individual strengths and audience needs and never defaults to a script or a canned speech.

The Enter, Enlighten, and Exit system outlined in this book will show you how to make an Entrance (Enter) into your subject matter, Enlighten your audience with the end goal in mind, and Exit or finish with purpose. The tools you will gain here may be applied when speaking before an audience of one or one hundred, or even in writing. You may apply the principles in the workplace, at the dinner table, and even online. A presentation or speech should always be thought of as a conversation. It's two-way, no matter how many people are in the audience or even if it's virtual.

The philosophies I reference throughout each chapter date back to Greek scientist and philosopher Aristotle. He was known as the "father of persuasion." And since most communication has some element of persuasion, his teachings are the perfect foundation for this book.

This book is about the basics. It's about learning to "read the music." Once you know the musical notes, you can begin to compose a melody that is unique to you. For some, this book is enough for now. For others, personal coaching is best to help them find their tune. Whatever works for you, I'm glad you're here.

> **Once you know the musical notes, you can begin to compose a melody that is unique to you.**

## How to Use This Book

To get the most out of this book, I recommend reading it through a first time in its entirety. Then go back through the book again and build your presentation, step by step.

You will notice that certain examples are referred to consistently throughout the book to show you how to do different things using the same presentation.

That's why it is extra helpful to read the book through in order the first time.

At the end of each chapter you will find a worksheet to help you collect your thoughts when designing a presentation. At the end of the book you will find a full workbook, where all the worksheets are compiled in the order that I use to create a presentation.

Feel free to use these worksheets any way you like. They are available in full-size PDFs at distinguished comm.com. There you will also find more examples and exercises. Examples are regularly added, changed, and updated. If you have trouble accessing these materials, go to distinguishedcomm.com/contact.

It takes practice, but once you get into the habit of using these tools, you will not only find it easier to construct a presentation, but you will be much more effective at doing so. If you keep at it, you'll start achieving incredible results.

# PREPARATION

Preparing for a formal presentation, a toast, or an important staff meeting is about much more than knowing the material. Preparation starts with asking yourself what the purpose of the communication is and how you will choose and organize the appropriate information to meet that purpose. This section will walk you through how to do that, step by step. And for those of you who experience fear when presenting, rest assured that when you have a clear goal and your information is organized in the way taught in this book, you'll find it will significantly tamp down those nerves.

# 1

# Setting Goals

You have a speech to give—*soon*—and you don't know where to start. Maybe it's a presentation of your firm's services to prospective clients. Perhaps it's a speech before the City Council arguing for a new park, or maybe before your team at work, letting them know about company changes.

How do you begin? Where do you start?

The first key to crafting a successful speech is to establish your goal—something that may involve more hard thinking than you first suspect. What are you trying to achieve with your presentation? Clients often tell us that their only goal is to "inform the audience." But think about this: if you are successful at "informing" the audience, what should the result of them having your information be?

In most cases, you want something to *happen* as a result of your presentation: prospective clients signing up for more information, colleagues being brought up to speed on revisions to the company website, tourists learning more about your town's history, and so on. Regardless of the subject of your presentation and the audience you are delivering it to, there is always an intended result that you are looking for.

If you're in sales, for example, the ultimate goal is usually straightforward: make a sale. And even so, closing the sale may not be the goal of a particular interaction. It may be simply getting your foot in the door with a lower-level person so that you can get an appointment with a higher-level person.

The crucial first step before presenting is to ask yourself what problem can you solve for your audience. How do you want the audience's thoughts or actions to change as a result of your communication?

But in many other interactions, identifying the goal is not as straightforward. Your goal does not need to be tangible. It may be to inspire certain feelings.

> **Every *meaningful* presentation should have a desired outcome.**

## What's in It for Them? (WIIFT)

Start by identifying what you have to offer your audience. That is what is meant by "know your audience." It doesn't help just to know that they are, for example, college-educated suburban dwellers, mostly ages 45–65. Find out in advance as much as you can about why they are likely to attend the meeting where you are going to present. Does the group have a common need you may address? Why should they listen to you? Talk to the organizer of the meeting and any key leadership to get these answers. The only way to give an audience what they want is to find out what that is.

Remember that human beings are, for the most part, selfish. We have little patience for wasting our time or money. When you are in front of an audience, even if the audience is only one person, they will be thinking, at least at some level, What am I getting out of this? Is this worth my time? Am I getting value?

So, as you prepare, identify what you are giving them. Just wanting them to know is insufficient. Force yourself to pinpoint what's in it for *them*. What value are you offering? And *that* should be the focus of the presentation.

## Example A: Pierce Airlines

Alex is the community outreach manager for Pierce Airlines. She initially may think that her only goal for an upcoming community meeting is:

> "To inform the local community about Pierce Airlines' neighborhood programs."

But thinking about WIIFT, she should add:

> "so that the community will have a good feeling about our airline and want to buy tickets from us rather than from the competition."

Even if Alex's job title at the airline is not "sales," an airline is a business. That means sales is part of everyone's job. Her job as community outreach manager is ultimately to create goodwill in the community, so they'll like Pierce Airlines more than the competition and buy tickets.

Alex can advise her audience of the large contributions the airline makes to local animal rescues or to school programs. She may tell them about community activities that the airline is involved in and volunteer opportunities that the audience can participate in.

But she also has an opportunity to make the audience *feel good* about flying with Pierce. By flying with Pierce, the community can feel that they are helping to rescue animals or provide disadvantaged children with school supplies. What's in it for them is feeling good. That should be the focus of Alex's presentation. What's in it for Pierce is increased ticket sales in the region.

> **What benefits will the audience gain by listening to you?**

## Example B: Human Resources

Amit is a human resources manager in a large company. His boss asks him to present data to all company supervisors regarding employee absenteeism over the past twelve months, its negative impact on productivity, and ways to increase attendance.

If Amit prepares for this presentation without much forethought, his planning will probably run along these lines:

In my presentation today, I will cover:
- Employee absenteeism over the past twelve months
- Negative impacts of absenteeism on productivity
- Ways to increase attendance

That approach disregards WIIFT. What's in it for the audience of supervisors? Will they benefit from increased productivity if employee absenteeism is down? How might an increase in productivity make them *feel*? Might they feel calmer? Less stressed? Is there a financial advantage for them?

If Amit wants his presentation to have a real impact, he needs to spell out the benefits of decreased absenteeism to his audience. *That* should be the focus of his presentation.

For example, he may discuss how supervisors would be less stressed if they could rely on employees showing up. Increased attendance by employees would mean fewer instances when supervisors have to step in to fill absent positions so they may feel better about their jobs. Perhaps there is a cash or time-off incentive for teams with the highest attendance.

Here is an alternative approach Amit might take (depending on the benefits he identifies):

I'm here to tell you how you can:
- Reduce your stress
- Feel better about your job
- Earn extra benefits

With this outline, Amit can fill in the same details and information but from a different angle. As he presents the challenge of absenteeism and how to address it, he also presents the *benefits* of addressing the problem to the audience.

# Goal-Setting Planner

What do I hope to achieve with
this presentation?

Who is my audience? What is
in it for them (WIIFT)?

**2**

# Organizing the Information

Enter, **Enlighten, and Exit** (EEE) is my proven method of presentation organization. Whether you are addressing an issue with your boss for three minutes or giving a one-hour keynote speech, the EEE model will serve you well. Here's what it means:

**Enter** the presentation with a bang!
**Enlighten** your audience.
**Exit** like a pro.

The model's three components—Enter, Enlighten, and Exit—each require their own distinctive methods of preparation and organization, which is the subject of this chapter. We'll first take a look at how to organize the information in an effective way so we can Enlighten the audience. Enlighten is the meat of the program, so let's address it first.

# Enlighten

Presentations are about imparting information, receiving information, and possibly persuading an audience to think or do something differently than they may have previously. This is why I view presentations as an opportunity to *Enlighten* your audience about a new idea, a project direction, or services available.

Just because you know a lot about a subject doesn't mean that you have to impart every bit of your knowledge to the audience in one sitting. There's only so much you can expect people to absorb at once. First, let's talk about how to get organized. Then we will go through an actual example.

## Organize Your Information into 3 Categories

I recommend grouping your message into three key points. Whatever your objective is, find a way to fit the information into three areas. Why three? Because the number three is magic and it works. Two is too few and four is too many.

> **Group your ideas into 3 categories.**

Aristotle created the Rule of 3 as the most effective way to organize information. Three pieces create the simplest pattern possible. Think about everything that comes in threes, such as children's fairy tales, the Trinity, and baseball! The Latin phrase *omne trinum perfectum* means everything that comes in threes is perfect, or every set of three is complete.

Getting all your content into three categories may sound impossible at first, but it can be done and gets easier with practice. To demonstrate, let's imagine that you are in charge of a client update on a large construction project. You meet with the client (often called the "owner") every two to four weeks to provide a project status. Here's how you organize the information into three groups for the next meeting:

## Step 1: Setting Goals

As described in chapter 1, first start with the goal. Ask yourself: Why am I making this presentation? What do I want out of it? What is my goal? What's in it for the audience? Why do they need this information? What am I offering? Remember, the answer is not "just to update the client." There must be an actual goal so that the presentation may be designed around that goal.

If you are a construction project manager tasked with giving the client an update. Your goals may be to:

- Ensure that the client is fully briefed on all items, positive and negative, so the client **feels confident** that you are thorough.

- **Allay any fears** from the client that the project will be delayed or less than expected.

- Create or **enhance the relationship** between the client and your company so that the client wants to work with you again.

## Step 2: Brainstorming

Next, brainstorm everything that is important to communicate and write it all down in no particular order (key words or ideas are easiest).

Departure of a key engineer

Mayor's tour

Pro bono work on homeless shelter

New person in that role

Difficulty sourcing glass

Pandemic impacts

Extreme weather at site causing delays

Contractor barbeque— owner invited

Power grid challenge

Current project schedule

Community event this weekend

Groundwater issue

## Step 3: Grouping

Group that brainstormed list into three main areas that seem to belong together. There is no right or wrong here as long as it makes sense. Here's one way you can do it:

### Stuff dealing with people

Departure of a key engineer

New person in that role

Pandemic impacts

### Timing & scheduling items

Difficulty sourcing glass

Extreme weather at site causing delays

Current project schedule

Power grid challenge

Groundwater issue

### Community & events

Mayor's tour

Pro bono work on homeless shelter

Community event this weekend

Contractor barbecue-owner invited

## Step 4: Naming

Once you've grouped the information into three sections, it's time to give each of those areas a name. Get creative if you are inclined. Below, the presenter listed some different names that each section could be called.

STAFFING—PEOPLE—PERSONNEL
Departure of a key engineer
New person in that role
Pandemic impacts

SCHEDULE—TIMELINE—CALENDAR—PROGRAM
Difficulty sourcing glass
Extreme weather at site causing delays
Current project schedule
Power grid challenge
Groundwater issue

COMMUNITY OUTREACH—PUBLIC—
SUPPORTING COMMUNITY
Mayor's tour
Pro bono work on homeless shelter
Community event this weekend
Contractor barbeque-owner invited

As you can see, there are multiple possibilities for section titles. I like that there happen to be three that start with the letter S, so if it were my presentation I would choose:

STAFFING
SCHEDULE
SUPPORTING COMMUNITY

I prefer section names that have something in common. If they all start with the same letter or rhyme or are all verbs, the audience can key in and remember the presentation better. This is not necessary, but something to strive for as you become well practiced at organizing your information in this way.

Reminder: There are no wrong answers here. You may group your topics any way you like and call them anything—as long as they make sense to you and will make sense to your audience! You could also name them People, Program, and Public.

Depending on which titles you choose, your presentation outline could look like this:

1. STAFFING
   a. Departure of a key engineer
   b. New person in that role
   c. Pandemic impacts

2. SCHEDULE
   a. Difficulty sourcing glass
   b. Groundwater issue

    c. Extreme weather at site causing delays
    d. Power grid challenge
    e. Current project schedule

3. SUPPORTING COMMUNITY
    a. Mayor's tour
    b. Pro bono work on homeless shelter
    c. Community event this weekend
    d. Contractor barbeque-owner invited

Notice that two of the sections have more than three sub-points. That's OK. What is most important is that you have only three *main* points. How much detail you go into for each of the three key points will depend on what you are trying to achieve and how much time you have. After going through the brainstorming and grouping processes, you may realize that you want more or fewer details in certain areas.

What is most important when developing your specific content is to stay focused on the goal. Don't default into telling the audience everything you know just because you know it. Focus on what is necessary to communicate in order to achieve the outcome you want. Some sub-points may require several minutes, while others may require only several seconds. For more on timing, see Exhibit A on time allotment later in the chapter.

More examples are available at www.distinguished comm.com.

## Enter

There is a big difference between just *starting* a presentation and actually *Entering* it with a BANG! This means that the very first things you say and do will set the tone for your entire presentation. It's not about being loud or flashy. An effective Entrance allows you to capture attention. With the EEE system, your Entrance cues the audience that you are worth listening to. It is a completely different approach than just introducing yourself and your topic. Listen to any great speaker and you will see a professional entrance.

> **The very first things you say and do will set the tone for your entire presentation.**

Let's return to the construction update example. A typical start for that sort of presentation would sound something like this:

"Hello. I'm Jordan, and I'm here to update you on the project. As you can see on our agenda, we will cover X, Y, Z."

Here is an example of the same introduction but rewritten as an entrance:

"Walt Disney once said, 'You can dream, create, design, and build the most wonderful place in the world. But it requires people to make the dream a reality.' At ABC joint venture, we are making our collective dream of this project a reality; and it's happening because of the incredible people out there working each day in this wonderful community. Today, I will share with you how our people are managing the work and the current schedule, and how we are reaching into the community."

Do you see how Jordan grabbed the audience's attention right from the start by using the quote from Walt Disney? The quote sets the stage for the audience in a creative way. He then uses the concepts in the quote to transition into the construction project to be discussed. Rather than just naming the agenda topic, this innovative start of the presentation is what makes it an Entrance.

Let's try another example. Imagine you're a firefighter who is presenting to a community group about pool safety. If you didn't put much thought into your presentation, you could well start with something mundane and passive like:

"Hi, I'm Nanci Joy, and I'm here from the fire department to talk to you about pool safety."

This is a typical start for this kind of presentation, but I find it boring.

An intentional entrance would sound something like this:

> "What would it take for you to feel safe enough to have your kids near a pool? Do you know about all the protections available to you and your neighbors to ensure that no child gets into a pool by accident? My name is Nanci Joy and here is how we can make our community safer together."

This grabs the audience's attention right from the start with questions that are relevant to the subject at hand. Questions, even if rhetorical, cause the audience to be active thinkers rather than passive listeners. And these particular questions likely speak directly to the concerns of the audience at this particular meeting. It's a small but important shift in approach.

## Enter with a BANG!

Other Entrance possibilities include starting with a story that establishes the framework for your message. For example:

> "I'd like to tell you about a homeless boy named Cooper. He was matched with an adult mentor at age nine. Over the years, Cooper spent lots of time with his mentor, Braden, an architect.

He visited Braden at work numerous times and saw what architects do and became very interested. His sophomore year of high school, he did an internship at Braden's firm and realized that he had incredible talent. Young Cooper, once homeless and living in a shelter, is now attending Arizona State University's School of Architecture."

Isn't that a more effective way to Enter the topic than saying:

"I'm here to tell you about how you can be a mentor to at-risk kids. First, you must get fingerprinted. Next you need to . . ."

Starting with a question, even if rhetorical, might best set the stage for your presentation. Think about reading aloud a critical line from the report you are about to present, or an attention-grabbing statistic that will instantly resonate with your audience and their concerns.

Entrances can consist of more than just words. Several bars of music played before you even utter a word may establish the right mood and create the launchpad you want. A demonstration of your product (if interesting) or an analogous demonstration of something else can be just what it takes to get the audience's attention riveted on you. For example,

Nanci the firefighter could start her presentation by lighting a candle, blowing it out, and asking:

"How can we be sure this candle is truly extinguished?"

After that, she could begin talking about the everyday causes of fires in that neighborhood, or something of similar concern to her audience. Do you see how compelling a well-designed entrance is compared to Nanci just stating her name and topic?

Visit www.distinguishedcomm.com for more ideas on how to Enter.

## Exit

Let's start with a key point of advice: Know when to stop!

It's such a shame when speakers are being really effective and then, when it's time to end, they simply don't know how. You will dramatically increase your effectiveness when you make a professional Exit. A professional Exit delivers a sense of closure to the audience and makes you stand out as a speaker in their minds.

Ineffective speakers end their presentations with any or all of the following or similar statements:

"Well, I guess that's it."
"Any questions?"

"Well, if there are no questions, I guess that's all."
"Thank you."
"So . . . uh . . . yeah."

None of those statements make a graceful Exit.

> ## Make a deliberate and intentional Exit.

A summary is also not a graceful Exit. You can give a summary, but then what? How do you actually *Exit?* It must be deliberate, or you'll end up saying one of those statements above. Although perfecting the art of Exiting could be the subject of an entire book, here we'll cover a few basic tips and pointers that will raise your game when it comes to knowing how to effectively conclude your presentation. Professional speakers will always finish with an Exit. Listen closely and you will hear them say something like:

"Let me leave you with this . . . "
"If you remember only one thing I said here today, remember this . . . "
"So the next time this happens, ask yourself . . . "

You can do the same thing at the end of your presentation, and it will make a world of difference. The power behind your message will be so much stronger if you deliver deliberate, final words that compel action rather than if you just say, "Thank you."

The same attention grabbers suggested for an entrance can also be used for an Exit. A story that brings everything full circle, several bars of music, or a demonstration can be just what it takes to Exit like a pro.

The firefighter could end her presentation two ways. Either she could repeat the lighting of the candle or she could let the candle stay aflame during the entire presentation. After she blows it out, she could say:

"How can *you* be sure this candle is extinguished?"

The possibilities are endless. Some famous Exits for speeches you may recognize include:

"Ask not what your country can do for you, ask what you can do for your country."
—John F. Kennedy, 1961

"Let us therefore brace ourselves to our duties, and so bear ourselves that, if the British Empire and its Commonwealth last for a thousand years, men will still say, **'This was their finest hour.'**" —Winston Churchill, 1940

"And when this happens . . . we will be able to join hands and sing in the words of the old Negro spiritual: Thank God Almighty, **we are free at last!**"  —Martin Luther King Jr.,1968

"Is life so dear, or peace so sweet, as to be purchased at the price of chains and slavery? Forbid it, Almighty God! I know not what course others may take; but as for me, **give me liberty or give me death!**"  —Patrick Henry, 1775

None of these speeches ended with "Any questions?" Once you've delivered your final line, *stop.* This is hard to get used to.

I recently attended a charity event where the keynote speaker was a very famous baseball player. He gave an outstanding speech and truly connected with the audience. It was clear that audience members were moved and motivated to make donations and get involved in the nonprofit that he was advocating for. Had he remained effective, the results could have been dramatic. But unfortunately, he did not know how to stop talking.

After a very impactful speech, he should have delivered a prepared Exit and asked the audience to donate or sign up. But instead, he just kept talking and saying things like:

"So once again . . ."
"Anyway, I guess that's really it . . ."

"As I said earlier . . ."

He was stuck in a vicious circle and could not get out of it. Instead of being focused on the incredible 20-minute speech, now the audience was in pain, watching him struggle. His inability to end his speech became the subject on everyone's minds, when they should have been reaching into their pockets. What a missed opportunity.

It takes a deliberate effort to say your final words and then be finished. This is why it is so important to be very clear about what those final words are before you get in front of your audience.

Your starting sentence and your ending sentence are the only things that I advise memorizing. Put a good clue or even the entire sentence for each in your notes.

## Time Allotment

Unless you are giving a keynote speech, you most likely have between 5 and 20 minutes to make your case. No matter what the time frame is, there are always presenters who say it's not enough. Here's the deal: it's the time you have been allotted, so how do you make the most of it?

For example, if you have been given 10 minutes, what can you realistically achieve in that time? Don't forget, first you need to grab attention with an Entrance, so let's say you decide to devote one of your 10 minutes to the Entrance. Now you have 9 minutes left for your *whole* presentation. What can you realistically communicate in 9 minutes? And how much time should you allot to each of the three groupings that constitute the Enlighten segment of your presentation?

There are many ways to approach this. You may decide to prioritize the Enlighten segment and thus spend only 30 seconds on your Entrance. Or, given the limited time you have to work with, you might determine that your presentation will be more successful if you prioritize a great Entrance. Here are two ways to divide up your 10 minutes. Both are right!

|  | Option A | Option B |
|---|---|---|
| **ENTER** | 30 seconds | 3 minutes |
| ENLIGHTEN<br>1.<br>2.<br>3. | 3 minutes<br>3 minutes<br>3 minutes | 2 minutes<br>1 minute<br>3 minutes |
| **EXIT** | 30 seconds | 1 minute |
|  | **= 10 minutes** | **= 10 minutes** |

EXHIBIT A

However you decide to split the time, the most important thing is that you stay focused on the goal and impart information that is most likely to help you to achieve that goal.

## Staying on Time

Keeping within the time limit is critically important. If your audience is expecting 10–15 minutes, they don't want 20–30 minutes. In fact, it's always a good idea to lean toward the lower end of the time given. What's more, you may be part of a larger agenda. That means if you take too much time, everyone after you on the agenda may have to cut their speeches short. Causing that type of disruption is likely to create frustration for the meeting planner, the other speakers, and the audience.

Using an outline rather than a script allows you to be flexible enough to adjust your speech on the fly. You may end up spending a lot less time on a particular area because the speaker before you already covered it. Or perhaps the speaker did not respect the time, and now yours has been cut in half so you have to adjust without notice. If you've ever served on a panel in front of an audience, you know this. It happens *all* the time, so plan for it.

Don't count on yourself to look at a clock while you speak. It's not reliable. The best way to stay on time is to find someone in the audience who can give you a signal(s) at designated time(s). Ideally, you should receive a signal about halfway through and again when you have just 1 or 2 minutes left. You decide the intervals that will work best for you.

Also decide whether you would respond best to someone subtly holding up fingers in the front row or a big sign in the back row. Most importantly, *take the cue.*

Even in a roomful of strangers, people are generally very willing to help with this task. Getting to the venue early will give you the opportunity to ask the moderator or a willing audience member to assist.

# ENTER-ENLIGHTEN-EXIT

. . . . . . . . . . . . . . . . . . . . . . . . . . . . . . . . . . . . .

**ENTER**
Start with a story, quote, catchy one-liner, question, demonstration—anything to grab attention—but not a topic sentence!

**ENLIGHTEN**
- Group all ideas into 3 main categories.
- Give each category a name.
- Create notes in outline form.
- Devise a plan to stay on time.

**EXIT**
End with a story, quote, catchy one-liner, question, demonstration—anything that says "I'm done." But don't end with a summary!

*A blank template is available for your use at www.distinguishedcomm.com.*

# 3

# Managing Fear

Most everyone has some fear or anxiety about presenting, even professional speakers, actors, and comedians. A certain amount of nervous energy is good. If you have none, you probably are not very invested in the material or you just don't care that much about having a successful engagement.

If you are feeling nervous about your upcoming presentation, ask yourself these questions to identify where your fear may be coming from:

- Do I know the material?
- Do I feel strongly about my message?
- Do I have a desired outcome?

If your answer to any of these questions is no, that could well be the cause of any typical, circumstantial nervousness about presenting that you are feeling. The remainder of this chapter will take you through a series of steps and exercises that will help you build confidence in yourself and what you have to say, dispel most if not all of your fear, and put you in a prime position to deliver a successful presentation.

Note: If your fear is *debilitating*, then it's important to try to figure out the root cause, as there is probably something else going on. A professional coach can help you to work through and strategically address this level of anxiety about presenting. In the meantime, the tactics discussed in this chapter will help mitigate *common* fear right now.

Managing presentation fear starts with understanding how we respond to fear in general. With that understanding, and with the tools we'll be discussing below, you'll be in a much better position to reduce the common fear associated with public speaking.

After learning about the brain and how to *command* your thoughts, we'll discuss how being in *control* of your environment and your delivery of the material can make an enormous difference when it comes to combatting fear. And finally, we'll talk about the body, how we are naturally wired to respond to fear and anxiety, and how to *change* those responses so they don't impair your ability to communicate effectively.

I call this method of managing fear Command, Control, and Change.

> **Fear is not alleviated by just "knowing the material."**

## Command Your Thoughts

- Focus on the goal. Remember this presentation is not about *you*; it's about the goal you have set out to achieve with your speech. This in turn means it's about communicating to your audience what's in it for them. (See chapter 1.)

- Visualize yourself doing a great job. The audience is loving it and you're having fun accomplishing your goal. (This is a common athletic technique that can be very effective.)

- Fear is not alleviated solely by "knowing the material." (If you don't know the material, you shouldn't be presenting it in the first place.) But you can alleviate fear related to the content by organizing your material in a productive way (see chapter 2) and by having supportive notes (see chapter 9).

- Many people are uncomfortable with silence, so our brains work to fill the void. That's why people say words like "uh," "um," "er," "well," "you know," "so," "like," and so on. Learning to be OK with silence is a skill. In fact, silent pauses during a speech can be very powerful because they give the audience a chance to process what was just said.

Another reason that people say "um" is that they are thinking about what to say next. It's OK to pause and think about what's next. But having organized material and notes will certainly help keep the flow going and avoid uttering filler words.

Using filler words during conversation is a habit many people have—and that habit needs to be broken. Asking a trusted friend to raise an eyebrow or give a signal each time you use filler words in daily conversation is a good way to get started. Don't wait until you are giving a presentation to do this. Break the habit in your everyday communication and it will translate to the stage.

More about the brain-body response to fear is covered in the body response section below.

### Control Your Environment

- Get to the venue early. Being rushed does not allow you to own the room and adds unnecessary anxiety. (See chapter 8 for more on this topic.) If you are delivering virtual presentations, sign on early for the same reason.

- Use notes (see chapter 9). Memorize the very first and the very last thing you plan to say and put a clue in your notes just in case. A clue is just a few keywords to jog your memory. For some reason, no matter how ready a presenter may be, remembering the first and last thoughts can be a challenge. This forgetfulness can occur due to the anticipation of starting or ending the presentation, both of which can increase adrenaline. As you'll see in chapter 9, I advise having only a keyword or two for each main point. But for your Entrance and your Exit, a little more detail is useful because of the nervousness that can happen in those moments.

- Don't drink caffeine or carbonated or icy drinks for two hours before an engagement. They can be hard on the vocal chords. Have room-temperature water or decaffeinated tea nearby.

- If you race through your words when you're nervous, try talking in slow motion. When you are that nervous, what feels like slow motion to you will actually sound like normal pace for the audience. (Seriously! Try it!)

- Another way to avoid speaking too quickly is to get in the habit of taking an intentional deep breath after every thought. Practice doing this in your everyday conversations to get into the habit. If you wait until presentation time to try it, you won't have established the habit and likely won't remember to do it.

> **If you race through your words when you're nervous, try taking a deep breath between thoughts.**

- If nerves creep up on you while you're talking, turn the next thing you were going to say into a question. Instead of saying, "We have 19 locations around the world," ask the audience, "Any idea how many locations we have?" By asking this question, you have introduced a customary pause in the conversation to allow listeners a chance to chime in with the answer.

And if you still need another few moments to relax or to think about your next point, just ask the audience another question! "In what countries do you think we have offices?"

> **Turn facts into questions.**

When presenting online, when you may not be in a position to actually take feedback vocally, you can still ask the questions, pause, and answer them yourself. This gives you time to breathe, and it also engages the audience by bringing them into the presentation. If there are a lot of participants, use the chat function to take responses from the audience.

## Change Your Body

- Change the nervous physiology of your
  body. Before you discount this approach,
  note that most people don't do this properly until they understand how it works.
  There are many schools of thought on the
  mind-body connection. Some believe that
  we have 100% mind control over everything happening in our bodies, including
  the ability to cure our own cancer through
  positive thinking. Others believe that we
  have zero ability to impact our bodies with
  our brains.

For our purposes here, let's stick with some basic
science. We are mammals, and that means we have
some things in common with other warm-blooded
vertebrates, including a fight-or-flight response. This
physiological reaction is what happens automati-
cally in our bodies when we're faced with real or perceived danger and physically prepares our bodies
to handle the threat. Our bodies release hormones
like adrenaline, which can cause increased heart
rate, rapid breathing, and tense muscles and can
lead to trembling. Anyone who has been told in this
situation to "relax" or "take deep breaths" has likely
found that this advice doesn't work well. But if you
relax and breathe correctly, you can short-circuit the

fight-or-flight response and avoid suffering the symptoms above.

Our first response if feeling threatened is to protect
ourselves. (And yes, giving a presentation can most
certainly be perceived as threatening.) In this situation, any mammal that can't run away will attempt to
hide from its prey and blend into the environment so
as not to be noticed, or it may even surrender.

One way to hide or blend in is to become "small"
or compact. In fear of danger, we're also likely to
slouch, or cover our necks or genitals, the most vul-
nerable areas of attack, as seen in these three photos.
These are our normal reflexes when we sense danger.

There is scientific evidence that you can interrupt this messaging between the brain and the body and lessen these nervous behaviors. Imagine a one-way street, where the brain is sending messages to the body. Your objective is to change the direction so that the body is sending messages to the brain instead. By doing the following, you will send messages to the brain that everything is OK and that the fight-or-flight response is unnecessary.

- Stand up straight with your chest out and shoulders back, arms at your side or on your hips.
- Take at least five long, deep breaths, counting "one Mississippi, two Mississippi, three Mississippi" the whole way as you

breathe in and again the whole way as you breathe out.

- Smile as wide as you can, five times for five seconds each time.

- Repeat this sequence at least three times, if possible. One of the reasons some may think that this type of approach doesn't work is that they give up after a breath or two.

By taking these steps, you are essentially tricking the brain. Imagine thinking, Wait a second. If I'm standing up straight and open, there can't be any danger. I couldn't be breathing this deeply if there were danger and I certainly wouldn't be smiling. If you are persistent enough, eventually, the brain will say, "I guess everything is OK!" and allow your body to relax.

This is not to say that all nervousness will disappear if you do this. But if these exercises are done in a focused and intentional way, you can absolutely lessen the hormonal response and resulting physiological symptoms. I do this several times in the room where I'm presenting before people start arriving (because I get there early!). Then I go into the restroom just before my presentation and do it again in private.

Practice doing these things regularly, whenever you can, to get your body used to them. Then, when you get to presentation time, your body will already be accustomed to benefiting from these tools. They will be way easier to do before a presentation. Not only that, but your body will be so well trained that you will be able to do them to some extent *during* your presentation. It may look to the audience that you are just taking a deep breath, but your brain will know that this is what you've trained for.

- Pacing or swaying can also be a challenge for nervous presenters. You may not even be aware that you do it. I believe that this, too, is part of the fight-or-flight response because we want to be ready to run at any moment. Moving around or keeping weight on only one leg allows you to run faster than if both feet are firmly planted on the ground.

The gentleman below is standing in a way that is very common during presentations, especially for men. It is an attempt to look casual but doesn't come off that way. Hands in pockets are never a good idea for a presentation. Not only does it tie up a hand, but keys or change in the pocket can create unintended noise and accentuate fidgeting. Notice he is leaning on one leg, subconsciously ready to run away if necessary.

Practice standing with your feet about hip-width apart, with equal weight on each foot. Place your empty hands at your sides, ready and available to express yourself. Practice this while waiting in the coffee shop line, standing at the water cooler, or chatting with a friend. Teach your body to be comfortable in this stance. Then aim for this as your base position while presenting. It will give you a body position to call "home" and will increase your awareness about nervous movement.

Practice all these fear-busting moves regularly. Think of them as weight training at the gym. If you're not trained to bench 200 pounds, you likely can't do it on command. But if you are trained and you keep up with that training, you'll be ready to bench that weight at any time.

## A Case Study in Managing Fear

I'd like to share the first time I saw a student make a major transformation using the Command, Control, and Change tools to manage her fear. Sometime in the early 2000s, a secretary for a large organization participated in my training. Jessica came to the training because she was largely responsible for making slide presentations for the managers, and it was helpful for her to understand what the presenters were learning.

Jessica was beyond terrified to present in front of a group, and she seemed ready to pass out when she realized that this was going to be a part of the training. When the time came for her first practice, Jessica nervously approached the front of the room. The tension was palpable, but everyone was rooting for her. And then, she did it. She made her presentation. And she was incredible. Her message was clear, she held our attention, and we gave her a standing ovation.

Upon returning to the safety of her chair, she told the group that she was so nervous, her knees were shaking and she could barely think. She was shocked to learn that no one could even detect that, as her performance was so seemingly comfortable. In fact, it looked as though she enjoyed it. Over the course of the seminar, Jessica practiced several more times and got better and more comfortable each time. Based on the feedback from the group, she realized that she was a truly excellent presenter.

After that, Jessica began to seek out opportunities to present wherever she could, just to get more practice. She spoke at secretarial meetings, at charities she was involved in, and at her church group. She committed to the Command, Control, and Change process of managing her fear because she was still very nervous. She says that she still relies on this process to this day.

Before every presentation and even before a potentially difficult phone call, Jessica takes command of her thoughts by thinking about the goal and purpose of the communication. This helps her to stay focused on why she is there and to remember that the communication is not about her but about what she is trying to achieve.

She is religious about ensuring that her nervousness doesn't take over her body by changing her breathing. She begins managing her breathing on her way to the venue and she continues to do it during preparation and even when she is being introduced.

Her most relied-on tool to control her environment is to ask the audience a lot of questions, pulling the focus off of her for a moment and giving her a chance to steady her breathing.

> **Asking the audience questions gives her a chance to breathe.**

Jessica's commitment to the Command, Control, and Change process, as well as her taking on lots of opportunities to practice it, has really paid off. She applied for a big promotion that would involve a lot of public speaking—and she got the job. Jessica transitioned from a lifelong career in secretarial work to the professional side of the organization.

We are still in touch after all these years. Jessica is now retired, but she still is speaking at her church and is always tapped to emcee events because she is so great in front of a crowd! She says she still gets nervous, but it's not debilitating, and the nervous energy actually makes her excited now.

Although this may sound like a fairy-tale example of managing public speaking fear, it's more common than you might think. I've seen numerous students make enormous transitions in public speaking, once they have the right tools to do so.

# Managing Fear

............................................

- Focus on the goal.

- Get there or sign on early.

- Use notes.

- Avoid caffeine and ice.

- Breathe between thoughts.

- Ask questions to create pauses.

- Stand up straight, shoulders back, feet hip-width apart.

- Prep with deep breathing exercise.

# PERSUASION

The keys to persuasion, according to Aristotle are logos, ethos, and pathos. Logos translates to "words" or "logic"; ethos means "credibility"; and pathos is "emotion" or "passion." We cover logos in the early chapters when we talk about how to logically organize the words for your presentation. Ethos is covered in various chapters as we discuss how you can confidently convey information as a credible source. This comes through not just the credentials in your bio, but by how and where you present yourself and how you behave before, during, and after a presentation.

Persuasion is impossible without logos and ethos, but they are nothing without pathos. The passion that you have for your subject and your ability to stir the emotions of your audience will make the difference between a persuasive or a non-persuasive presentation.

For far too long business presenters have ignored the third component of Aristotle's secret to persuasion, and only focused on logos and ethos. What we now know in this era of new appreciation for storytelling and programs like TED Talks, is that pathos is just as important. We must connect to our audience through emotion if we want to make an impact and be persuasive.

**4**

# Impact Through Emotion

## Rationalizing

Effective presenters deliver information *and* tap into emotions—their own and those of their audience. Facts and figures will take you only so far. Your audience will really connect with the subject matter through their emotions—how they *feel* about what you are saying. This understanding goes all the way back to Aristotle and his teachings on the value of the *emotional appeal*. He believed in "persuasion through passion." Logic and reason have their role, but it is feelings that ultimately drive action. Emotion must be at the core of your message: love, fear, pity, anger, surprise, excitement, honor, shame, and so on.

One of the biggest mistakes that communicators make is focusing only on data when presenting. Numbers, charts, and graphs dominate their presentations, yet no matter how impressive those numbers are, the speaker is ineffective. The audience is unmoved.

We like to think that we make decisions based on reasonable facts. Aristotle's premise is that we make decisions based on emotion and then *justify* those emotionally driven decisions with facts, logic, and reason.

For example, have you ever been on a diet? I sure have. Here's a typical diet week for me:

Days 1–2: I'm a perfect angel.

Days 3–5: I might cheat a tiny bit, but I'm sticking to it.

Days 6–7: I'm getting pretty tired of the whole thing. And like most diets, mine usually start on Mondays. By the weekend, I'm in real need of some serious carbs and sugar. So begins the typical rational-versus-emotional brain struggle.

My rational brain wants to stick to a diet. My emotional brain wants some sugar! Which side do you think usually wins? Here is the push-pull "conversation" that happens in my brain:

| FIGHTING CONVERSATIONS IN THE BRAIN ||
| RATIONAL BRAIN | EMOTIONAL BRAIN |
| --- | --- |
| I'm meeting friends for dinner at my favorite burger joint, but I'll just order a salad. | We'll see about that. Those french fries are really good. |
| I was so good all week. A few fries won't hurt. | All the food is smelling so good here. I'm starving! |
| I haven't had anything but vegetables in six days. I deserve to eat a burger and fries with my friends. | This tastes amazing. I love this so much. This feels so good. I'm so happy right now. |
| I'll start my diet again tomorrow. | Food wins. |

**FACTS**
Added weight is a contributor to heart disease and diabetes.
French fries are fattening.
Fried food contributes to weight gain.
People eat for reasons other than hunger.

EXHIBIT B

The emotional brain identifies feelings that the rational brain justifies and ultimately gives in to (usually). The facts are important but are not controlling the narrative. Understanding this about your audience is critical when presenting information that you want them to absorb and possibly act on. Facts, figures, and rational arguments won't touch their hearts and cause them to act. Facts alone are not persuasive.

Think about commercials that show children living in extreme hardship or abused animals in need of rescue. This is a deliberate effort designed to elicit the viewers' emotions. People either *feel* something or turn the ad off because they don't want to feel something. The ads don't rely on presenting numbers and statistics alone. They show powerful images of babies and puppies and then ask if *you* want to make a difference. The aim is to *connect* with you and to empower you to make a difference. They want you to *feel for* and identify with those who need your help.

> **Feelings ultimately drive action—
> not logic and reason alone.**

## Storytelling

Imagine you are attending a presentation about the 2020 pandemic and the presenter says, "More than 3200 people died today of COVID-19." While your rational brain would likely be cognizant of how big that number is, would that information have a true emotional impact on you? Likely not.

But if the presenter added a story about a specific individual whom people could relate to and feel for, the presentation is transformed from being about numbers to being about human beings. This greatly improves the chances that the audience will connect to the information. For example:

> "Dan, a 42-year-old veterinarian, was well known in his community for treating every animal like it was his own pet. He loved going hiking with his wife and children and took in countless stray, sick animals that the family encountered on their hikes. He would bring them back to health and then rehome them with loving families. Dan was perfectly healthy, with no underlying conditions. Then he got sick for a few days and figured he would be fine. But yesterday things got much worse and he started struggling to breathe, seemingly out of nowhere.

> "COVID-19 took his life today. His 6-year-old daughter and 9-year-old son will never see their dad again. And Mary, the love of his life and wife of 12 years, is now a single mother. Dan and more than 3,000 other souls died today, and another 3,000 are likely to die tomorrow from COVID-19."

One of the reasons storytelling is so powerful is that it allows the audience to put themselves in the shoes of the characters; to identify with them and to feel for them. It is one of the most powerful ways to connect with the audience. Moving forward in this book, storytelling should be thought of as one of the many "connectors" available to you in presenting.

> "People will forget what you said; people will forget what you did; but people will never forget how you made them *feel*."
> —Maya Angelou

## Using the Senses

In addition to feelings like happiness, sadness, pride, and so on, connection can be achieved through the five senses. Suppose you are an architect presenting information about a new building. The audience can *look* at your endless slides of floor plans, renderings, and high-tech security systems. But what else could you add to tap into their *feelings and senses?*

Here are some ideas:

- Provide a piece of the actual tile adorning the new building for people to *touch.*
- Play the sounds of the birds that visitors will *hear* in the new courtyard garden.
- Bring in a bouquet of the same type of flowers that they will smell in the garden.
- Read a quote from someone in the disabled community who is overjoyed (feelings)
- because he will now be able to access this new facility.
- Share samples from the ground-floor bakery for the audience to *taste.*

Connecting information to the audience's senses adds depth and a dynamic dimension to the communication that helps to make a lasting impact.

Imagine that you work for a nonprofit that helps homeless and troubled children by matching them with stable, adult volunteers. Your job is to recruit willing adults to become mentors, typically through live, in-person presentations. This subject matter provides countless options to make an emotional impact on and persuade the audience. In addition to slides of kids and mentors in action (slides will be discussed in chapter 5), think about all the other opportunities you have at your disposal to make a powerful presentation to your audience.

In concert with talking about the impact of mentoring on both child and mentor, the recruiter could integrate a specific experience. For example, a popular activity for mentors and youth is to go on group camping trips. Describing a camping trip experience provides infinite possibilities to appeal to the prospective volunteers' five senses. Many adults may have fond memories of sitting around a campfire as children and eating traditional camp food like toasted marshmallows or s'mores (toasted marshmallow with a piece of chocolate between two graham crackers). Here are a few presentation ideas just on the subject of s'mores!

- Bring a marshmallow on a skewer as a **visual** aid.

- Pass around (**touch**) a piece of burnt charcoal, encouraging the audience to smell it, perhaps reminding them of campfire memories.

- Prepare in advance a plate of s'mores for everyone to **taste** (using marshmallow cream, since you likely can't light a fire).

- Describe in detail the crackling fire or play a video (**sight**) of a crackling fire (**sound**).

Not only have you put the prospective volunteers into the headspace of that camping trip by more than just talking about it, you have actually enabled them to see, touch, smell, taste, and hear the experience using the tools above. As the recruiter proceeds to describe why these mentoring relationships and camping trips are so meaningful, the audience has a true connection to that experience. This is so much more powerful in making an emotional connection than using words and slides alone.

> **Feelings and senses are *connectors*.**

Let's look at another example of how to incorporate the senses into presenting. What if you want the purchasing committee to authorize the purchase of new software that would organize office workflow? You might focus on:

1. The current situation with disorganized office workflow
2. How the new software would get busy workflow organized
3. What success would look like

How can you incorporate feelings and senses into this subject? Let's take a look.

1. DISORGANIZED WORKFLOW

   - As you introduce the idea that the current workflow situation is very disorganized and *unclear*, you could ask an audience member to try on your glasses and tell everyone what they *see*. This is a visual demonstration.

   - In discussing how frustrating a disorganized workflow is, you could ask everyone to write their name with their nondominant hand. This is a tactile demonstration of experiencing frustration.

2. GETTING ORGANIZED

   - When describing the busy workflow, you could show a photo or video of bees in a beehive, where each bee has a specific job (this is a visual approach).

   - As you describe how easy it would be to enter the necessary data to organize workflow, you could conduct a live demonstration of the software or guide an audience member through doing it. This would activate both visual and tactile senses.

3.  SUCCESS

    - A chart could *visually* show how the company's numbers will increase.

    - You could conclude by saying something like "With this software, we will become as organized as those bees in the hive, increasing productivity dramatically. I can taste the success."

    - You could then pass out individual honey sticks sold at health food stores. This would reach the senses of taste, touch, and smell.

## Engaging Your Audience When Presenting Online

Engaging emotions, feelings, and senses is just as important when communicating online as it is in person, if you want to be persuasive. Being online means you need to make a slight shift in your approach. For example, since you can't offer anything in person, you won't be able to stimulate all the senses, so you must rely more on descriptive language and visuals. Using descriptive language to touch on all the areas described in this chapter can be just as effective online. And as you'll learn in chapter 5, there is more to using visuals than slides.

Depending on the importance of the meeting, you may even consider sending a physical package to participants in advance that contains sensory items.

The package could be marked: "Please do not open until the November 14 at 2 p.m. meeting." Inside the package might be the aforementioned bakery items to **taste**, tile samples to **see** and **feel**, and floral potpourri to mimic the **smell** of the flowers in the new garden.

Imagine how the group would feel if you did this? Rather than the usual video call with someone talking about all these things, now the audience can actually experience them. When you are talking about the snack bar, you can ask everyone to reach into their package, pull out the muffin, and taste it. Even though the audience is participating in a video presentation, they are more actively engaged.

Of course, this isn't always an option, because either mailing something in advance isn't feasible or the meeting is tomorrow and you're just now reading this book! How else can you connect to feelings and senses when you are behind a screen? Even on a video call, you can show real objects rather than just pictures on slides. Your holding the product, describing it, and perhaps even operating it can have a much greater impact than just a photo. Use sensory and descriptive language whenever possible. For example, when describing a product's finish, you could say, "When I touch this, it's a smooth as glass." Get creative. Have fun with it!

## Memory

Tapping into senses and emotions also helps with memory. For example, do you remember exactly where you were five Tuesdays ago at 9 a.m.? Most likely, you don't. But if you were at least five years old in 2001, you surely remember where you were on September 11 that year. The reason you remember is that you felt something strongly that day and those feelings connect to your memory.

Similarly, you likely recall your last group activities in early 2020 before you had to change your life due to COVID-19. You may have felt nervous, uncertain, anxious, or any number of other emotions. If you experienced emotions, you are more likely to remember the experiences themselves.

In the same vein, you may remember something specific about your first day of school, your first kiss, the death of a loved one. Minute details about the weather, a song that was playing, or what you had for breakfast would likely never be recalled on a non-eventful day. But when there is a strong emotional connection to the situation, your memory is likely to be stronger than ever.

When you want to make an impact on someone, persuade them, and/or increase your chances that they will solidify or change their thoughts or actions, you must touch their emotions.

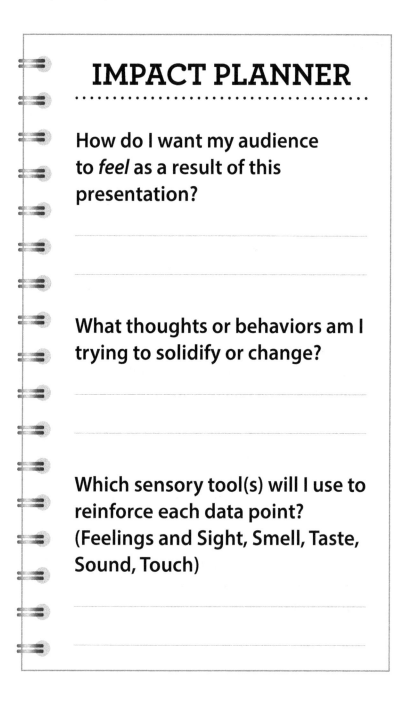

# IMPACT PLANNER

How do I want my audience to *feel* as a result of this presentation?

What thoughts or behaviors am I trying to solidify or change?

Which sensory tool(s) will I use to reinforce each data point? (Feelings and Sight, Smell, Taste, Sound, Touch)

# 5

# Visuals Should *Aid*

**A**n entire book could be devoted to the material in this chapter, but for now we will focus on a few changes you can make right away to dramatically increase the effectiveness of your visual aids.

As we discussed in the last chapter, presentations can be greatly enhanced by touching all the senses. In this chapter we will focus on sight, one of the most common connectors used in presenting, especially in a large crowd or over the internet. Visual aids offer an additional means of transmitting your message to your audience, allowing them to take in information above and beyond your words.

For example, you can verbally describe in detail what a new office building will look like, or you can do that *and* show drawings or photos of it. If it's important to your outcome that the audience can visualize the new building, it's your job as a presenter to provide whatever tools you can to help them do that.

## Visual Means *Visual*

Many speakers default to PowerPoint and other slide programs whenever they give a presentation. Before you do the same, ask yourself if slides will truly *add* to your presentation's message. Don't default to slides out of habit. Slide programs are meant to visually demonstrate your points as you are speaking. In other words, they were designed to showcase images and graphics, not words.

If you must put text on the screen, aim for a maximum of 5–10 words. Use the rest of the slide for photos or graphics that fill up the screen and can be easily seen. Remember, people in the back of the room will not be able to see your slides as clearly as you do when you are creating them on your computer. Make your images as big and clear as possible.

I am not suggesting that you attempt to limit the *number* of slides but that you limit the words on each slide. A five-minute presentation can have 20 effective slides that move along quickly. And a too-long presentation of 30 minutes can have five slides. This concept is not about the number of slides, but about how they are used to aid the audience in understanding the material.

## Do Your Visual Aids *Add* to Your Message?

All too often, I see presenters using visuals in their presentations that don't add any value to the message. They put something on a screen that they know people can't see and then say:

"I know you probably can't see this, but . . ."

Why do they do that? I guarantee that someone using visuals in the next three presentations you attend will do that. Don't let it be *you*.

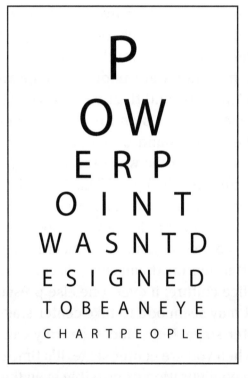

This "eye chart" is a good way to remember not to make your audience work at seeing your slides.

## Slides Are Wallpaper, Not the Main Event

Slides should *support* your points, not be written versions of your points. If your slide is full of lengthy text, it takes only a few seconds for the audience to dismiss it altogether because they are not going to read it. The opposite is true for images. Your audience can register image information so fast that they will look at the visual for a few seconds, be impacted by it, and then turn their eyes right back on *you*. If you are the presenter, acknowledge to yourself that *you* are the main event, not the slides.

Many presenters are under the impression that they can "hide" behind their visuals. They think that the audience will focus on the slides rather than on them. They often stand off to the side of the room so they won't be in the way of the screen, and some will even turn out the lights! This is an effort to "disappear" and not be the focus of the presentation.

Presenters do this for several possible reasons. The most common reason is concern about having all the attention on themselves. It can also be part of the office culture: if everyone else presents in the corner, it may seem odd to take center stage. Always take center stage. If the audience truly can't see the visuals when you are center stage, it's time to change the room configuration or possibly even find a different room. (See chapter 8.)

A similar issue occurs when presenting online. Presenters can choose to remain on screen, even while their visuals are showing. If they wish to hide, they can shut this feature off so that the only thing the audience sees is the slide. This makes the presenter just a voice, similar to what a live presentation in a dark room would be like.

Be clear on this: if you are presenting, *you* are the focus. You will fail if you attempt to make your visuals the focus of your presentation and hide behind them. Use visuals as *aids* only. Remember that the presenter is *you*, the living, breathing, talking human being. You are what the audience should pay attention to.

## Visual Aids Are *Not* Your Presenting Notes

Why do some presenters type out their notes, put them up on a screen, and then read them to the audience? Does anyone enjoy having a presentation read to them? What value is the presenter bringing to the audience in that scenario? If you are going to read words from a slide to the audience (while they look at your backside), then why are you there? Just give them a handout and let them read it on their own! They need to see your eyes and face to connect with you.

Ineffective presenters often say that they are relying on their slides so that they'll know what to say. Slides are not presenting notes. (We'll cover how to use notes in chapter 9.) If you are relying on your slides to tell you what to say, you are in big trouble when the slides fail!

## Have a Backup Plan

Don't ever rely 100% on electronic media for your presentation. Even if you test it moments before and everything works fine, it could fail at any time. Make sure you have a backup plan. Be ready to present without electronics, just in case.

Your backup plan should not necessarily be to bring printouts of your slides to hand out to everyone in the room. Consider developing a one-sheet of info-graphics, highlighting your main points, which can be used to complement your presentation. You could redirect your presentation to that document if the full slide show fails. It also serves as a nice takeaway.

Alternatively, if you have a web page, you could ask people in the room to log on and you could point to visuals there. In today's world, there's a good chance most people in the room have at least one eye (or thumb) on their phone. Why not ask if they'll join you in looking at a web page? If you have your phone logged on, ready to go and accessible on stage, you can grab it and direct the audience to a great photo on your site that relates to your point. In fact, it's not a bad idea to do this anyway!

> **If you are relying on your slides to tell you what to say, you are in big trouble when the slides fail!**

## Slide-Formatting Example

Let's look at an example of how to make a boring, wordy, useless slide into something useful. Below is a real slide that I found online from a university alumni association when I was doing some research for a university client. The only thing I changed was the name of the school and the mascot. Everything else is exactly as it was presented below.

---

### University Alumni Association – Goals

Increase alumni association membership

Enhance the alumni association's visibility in select regions, especially California, Texas and Florida

---------------------------------------

Develop a long-range plan for engaging young alumni

Sustain the operation of the Alumni Center through fund-raising and rentals

Increase student awareness of the alumni association through relevant programming and campus partnerships

---

EXHIBIT C

Who is going to read this slide during a presentation? The answer is likely no one. Knowing that slides are not presenter notes, what keywords would you pull out of this text to make it a more effective visual aid?

First, we strike out the superfluous words.

**University Alumni Association – Goals**

Increase ~~alumni association~~ membership

Enhance ~~the alumni association's~~ visibility in select regions, ~~especially California, Texas and Florida~~

--------------------------------------

~~Develop a long-range plan for~~ engaging young alumni

Sustain ~~the operation of the~~ Alumni Center ~~through fund-raising and rentals~~

Increase student awareness ~~of the alumni association through relevant programming and campus partnerships~~

EXHIBIT D

Focusing on only the key words above would result in this:

**University Alumni Association – Goals**

- **Increase membership**
- **Enhance visibility (in select regions)**
- **Engage young alumni**
- **Sustain Alumni Center**
- **Increase student awareness**

EXHIBIT E

Now it's time to group all the key ideas into three categories. There is no right or wrong answer, as long as it makes sense. The red arrows show what areas I feel go together best.

University Alumni Association – Goals

- Increase membership
- Enhance visibility (in select regions)
- Engage young alumni
- Sustain Alumni Center
- Increase student awareness

EXHIBIT F

Exhibit G shows those three key areas grouped together, using a photo background instead of white. That's still a lot more than three to five words on a slide and therefore not the most effective visual aid.

University Alumni Association – Goals

Enhance visibility
Increase membership

Engage young alumni
Increase student awareness

Sustain Alumni Center

EXHIBIT G

Here's what happens when I clean it up. We get three key areas and two of them happen to begin with the letter E. You could stop right there, but when the word "Energize" came to me, I had to go with it. See Exhibit I.

EXHIBIT H

Exhibit H, which shows three key points focused on Enhance, Engage, and Energize, is clearly stronger than the original slide we started with. But the questions are How does this slide *aid* visually? and What could be shown to visually aid each of these points?

Per the original slide (Exhibit D), the Alumni Association's goal is to increase membership and enhance visibility in California, Florida, and Texas. Exhibit I would be a better way to aid the viewers than the original slide.

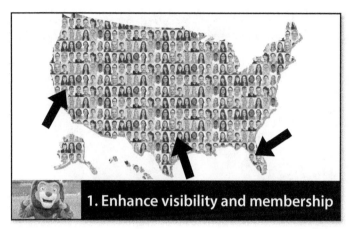

EXHIBIT I

Using the same philosophy for points 2 and 3 would result in slides that look more like these:

EXHIBIT J

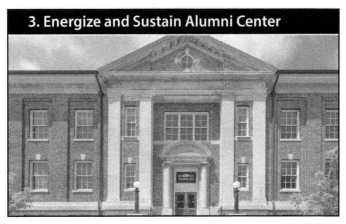

3. Energize and Sustain Alumni Center

EXHIBIT K

## Another Slide Formatting Example

Exhibit L is a real-life slide that I borrowed for this example (the name of the organization has been changed). Bob's Kids helps homeless and troubled children by matching them up with stable adult volunteers, and the organization is constantly looking for willing adults to volunteer as mentors. The slide is from a mentor recruitment presentation.

---

### Bob's Kids

- Through Bob's Kids, at-risk young people can succeed with the guidance of a volunteer mentor who has chosen to make a positive impact on a young person's life.
- Bob's Kids aims to empower youth to fulfill their potential through mentoring and life skills development.
- We are a model for what mentoring relationships can be in our community.
- Bob's Kids connects youth ages 7–17 with adult mentors to help kids reach their greatest possible potential. We have a curriculum that focuses on social and emotional learning. The curriculum involves programs through which youth acquire and apply knowledge, attitudes, and skills with the support of their mentors.
- Through Bob's Kids, volunteer mentors have transformed the lives of 9,600 youth through the development of social, emotional, and academic skills with the help of committed volunteers and community support.

---

EXHIBIT L

Imagine yourself as a prospective volunteer sitting in the audience for this presentation. Are you going to read this slide? Would you want the slide read to you? Of course not. What is the point of a slide like this? In most such cases, the presenter is using this type of slide as a crutch to tell them what to say and is not putting much, if any, thought into how the slide will help the audience. This presenter has likely never had good presentation training, or they wouldn't do this. (The next time you see a slide like this, please send the presenter my way!)

In my coaching sessions, I help participants to transform their presentations by moving away from using slides like the one above (or any other bad visuals) to using visual aids that will actually make an impact on the audience. Here's how I would enhance this slide's effectiveness.

I see three key points that can be extracted from the bulleted list in Exhibit L. I've put them into Exhibit M below. While I encourage no more than 5–10 words on any slide, the slide in Exhibit M is certainly better than the one in Exhibit L. To be clear, the presenter may *say* all the text in Exhibit L, but those words should never be written out, verbatim, on a slide for the audience to see. Instead, a text-only slide should show the audience only the essential messages you are communicating.

## Bob's Kids

① At-risk kids succeed with mentors

② Empowerment through life skills

③ Volunteering transforms lives

EXHIBIT M

As you can see, the important key ideas from the verbose slide are reflected here in a much clearer way. It's an improvement but still—believe it or not—too wordy. And it does little to connect with the audience's feelings.

As a prospective volunteer, what do you really want to *see*? How about real people just like you and the kids whom they are mentoring? The presenter has a visual tool at his fingertips. Why not use it to *show the audience* impactful visuals, instead of mere words?

Let's distill the message further. The keywords I see above are "succeed," "empowerment," and "transforms." If we change them slightly to "Success," "Empowerment," and "Transformation," we then have active, positive words that point to all the ideas in the original slide. When those three words are combined with effective visuals like those below in Exhibit N, the presenter can reinforce the key takeways while also telling stories about real people in the program. Who are these kids? What are they like? How would it feel to spend time with them? How do these mentors feel about their experiences?

EXHIBIT N

## Online

Although people sitting in the back of the room aren't an issue when you are presenting virtually, keep in mind that some participants may be looking on a phone screen or calling in with no access to visuals at all. Keeping words to a minimum will help those on a tiny screen, but how do you assist those just on the phone? For people who are calling in, take a moment to describe the visual to them so that they feel included.

**EXERCISE:** Visit www.distinguishedcomm.com for more slide transformation exercises.

## There's More to Visuals Than Slides

Can you think of any ways beside slides to visually demonstrate your points? Do you have any props? Could you perform a live demonstration? Is there an analogous process that's similar to what you're talking about that would help to make your point?

For the Bob's Kids example, the presenter should consider asking a real volunteer mentor and their young mentee to attend the meeting and share their experience in person. Although that may not always be possible, it would certainly make a much more powerful impact on the audience than just a photo.

A real mentor and mentee live and in the room, or on screen, are also visual aids. In fact, they're more than mere visual aids because their voices touch the sense of hearing in a way that a slide can't.

## Add dimension to your presentations.

Get creative and think about other ways to visually demonstrate your message. For example, if you are talking about how difficult providing evidence in a lawsuit is, you may say, "Producing evidence in this case is like finding a needle in a haystack."

Imagine if you started your presentation by actually searching for a needle in a small haystack! You could fill up a clear bowl with straw from a craft store, place a large, blunt needle inside, and use it to make your point as you search for it. (More about analogies and metaphors in chapter 6.)

If you are talking about materials used in a construction project, why not bring the actual materials for people to see and touch. Wouldn't that be more memorable than just photos?

Or when describing how difficult it is to choose a new computer, think of a comparison that may help explain that. You could demonstrate this with a box of chocolates. Ask a few people to quickly choose a piece from the box. Acknowledge the difficulty in doing so because people don't know what they are choosing. Does it feel a little like that sometimes when buying a computer?

Periodically, people will come to a seminar or reach out to me online and comment about a presentation they remember me giving years ago. It shouldn't shock me, because I know the strategies in this book work, but I do get a kick out of it every time that happens.

One speech in particular comes up a lot. I was the Phoenix Airport public relations manager at that time, and I was speaking to a full ballroom of airport managers from the southwestern United States at an aviation conference. As I recall, it took place in Monterey, California. I was asked to speak about the importance of airports having crisis communications plans.

In the years preceding the conference, a very popular antidrug advertising campaign featured someone holding two eggs. Some readers may remember the television ad that went something like this:

"This is your brain." (Actor shows the two eggs.)

"This is your brain on drugs." (Actor cracks the eggs into the pan and they begin to fry.)

My opening visual aid was a takeoff on this because I knew everyone in that room at the time would have been familiar with that campaign. As I recall (and as many have told me in the years following), my opening lines went something like this:

> "This is your airport." (I showed the audience two eggs.)

> "This is your airport without a crisis communications plan." (I cracked the eggs into the pan and stirred them up.)

I proceeded to explain the importance of having a crisis communications plan.

This all may sound very dramatic; and to be fair, there is certainly a dramatic element to the approach. What's most important to note is that it works. Watch and listen to effective speakers and you will see they utilize this technique often.

Now it's up to you to find visual aids that work for you. Think more broadly than slides. You'll be amazed at how creative you can be once you get into the habit of thinking this way.

# VISUAL AIDS PLANNER

Do I have notes for myself?

Are my slides easy-to-see visuals, with no more than 5 words?

Do I have a plan if the slides fail?

What visual aids will I use besides slides?

# 6

# Examples, Comparisons, and Questions

Once you are comfortable tapping into emotions and utilizing visual aids successfully, there is even more that you can do to be persuasive, make your presentations stand out, and your messages stick. Your audience must be able to relate to your information and have an opportunity to process it in their own minds. Using examples, comparisons, and questions will help them to do so. These are all powerful connectors.

## "For Example": The Key to Helping Your Audience Understand

It's one thing to introduce an audience to a theory, a process, a new invention, and so on by using carefully chosen words to describe it. But to make an unfamiliar concept into a familiar concept, to really make it "stick," using *examples* is critical. We are wired to be wary of the unfamiliar as a matter of survival. For example, ask most toddlers to try a new food and see what happens.

Explaining how an economy works to someone of any age can be challenging, especially if using typical language for the subject, such as "An economy is a system for allocating resources to meet people's needs and wants and is strongly determined by the amounts of both supply and demand."

A first-timer to the concept of the economy would surely have a better chance of understanding it if the dry explanation presented above was supplemented with a relatable example, such as:

> "A local grocery store is a mini-economy. The buyer for the store decides what customers in that area are most likely to buy and how much they are likely to pay. The store then puts products on the shelves [supply] and sets prices based on how much a customer would be willing to spend [demand]."

You can take it a bit further with another example:

> "Imagine pineapples are regularly $4 each and suddenly there is a shortage of pineapples due to a drought. As a result, the grocer is able to obtain only a few pineapples to sell [supply]. The customers who really want those few

pineapples are likely to pay $6 or more just to get one [demand]."

Unfortunately, most speakers weaken their presentations by only giving general information without further illustrating their points with examples. Take a look at these three unrelated cases of *not* giving examples:

a. "Our organization deals with infectious diseases all the time."
b. "At Bob's Kids, we help homeless kids to discover what their lives could be like."
c. "I'm very adept at dealing with difficult employees."

As you can see, these assertions convey the basic information but certainly don't do much else to make an impression. What do you think would really help the audience to relate to these points? *Examples*, of course! The speaker should give specific examples that enable the audience to better connect with what is being said. If each point were followed by the words "for example" and then an informative verbal illustration to bolster the point, the audience would be much more likely to understand and connect to the information.

> ## Two of the most important words in any communication are "for example."

Just like right now, as you are reading this, we could stop short by only giving you the information in the paragraph above and moving on to the next section. But wouldn't it be more helpful to give you *examples* of how to do it? Each of the three points above is now followed with an example to support it:

a. "Our organization deals with infections diseases all the time."

"*For example*, we were the lead health agency during the Ebola outbreak of 2014, and we were responsible for creating and executing the first infectious disease response in the US in modern-day history. We have been at the forefront of every health crisis around the world ever since."

b. "At Bob's Kids, we help homeless kids to discover what their lives could be like."

"*For example*, Cooper visited his mentor at work numerous times as a teenager and saw what architects do and became very interested. His sophomore year of high school he did an internship at the firm and realized that he had incredible passion for this type of work. He is now attending

Arizona State University's School of Architecture."

c. "I'm very adept at dealing with difficult employees."

"*For example*, a few years ago I had an employee who was an excellent worker but a terrible team member. Apparently, no one had ever disciplined her in the past because she was so productive. She got moved to my area so I could 'handle' her. We worked together to set ground rules and created a detailed performance plan for which I held her accountable. Today, she is an excellent team member, leader, and a true example of how people can learn, change, and grow."

## Comparisons Make Information Easier to Grasp

Sometimes, the easiest way to explain something complicated or to make it memorable is to compare it to something else that is familiar to the listener. Idioms, similes, metaphors, and analogies all offer ways to do this. Don't worry if you don't remember these terms from your high school English class. Just look for opportunities to draw parallels between what you are discussing and something that would be easily familiar to the audience. Comparisons enable you to take complex subjects and simplify them. Here are some examples of how to do it. Notice how much more complete the communication is when these tools are used.

"When I was first assigned this project, I panicked."

Add: "I felt like I was handed a thousand-piece puzzle in a blank box. I had no idea where to begin."

"It was so foggy; you couldn't see anything."

Add: "It was like being in a white-out blizzard in Alaska!"

"Employee investment is the lifeblood of a healthy company."

Add: "Getting rid of employee investment to save costs is like losing weight by giving blood."

"I don't think she can keep this up for much longer."

Add: "A stone may skip a long way, but it always sinks, eventually."

"He keeps making these little mistakes, which are adding up."

Add: "A leaky boat is a sinking boat."

"We sell over 60,000 cakes a year."

Add: "Imagine that the cakes we sold last year could fill every seat in a Super Bowl football stadium."

"People suffered from severe loneliness during COVID-19."

Add: "Social isolation can be as damaging to health as smoking 15 cigarettes a day."

## Questions Help Your Audience to Engage

Questions are a highly effective way to engage the audience, even if the question is rhetorical. There is an enormous difference between delivering information to the audience without interacting with them and engaging the audience with questions that will get them *thinking* about what you are saying. The brain is put into a state of active engagement when a question is asked.

For example, you may say: "We sell over 60,000 cakes a year." And the audience will politely stare at you.

Or you could ask, "How many cakes do you think we sell each year?" Now the audience's brains are churning as they contemplate the task you've assigned them. Now they are truly engaged.

This is not to say that every piece of information should be presented in question form. Rather, consider asking questions as a tactic to use occasionally to stay connected to the audience.

Adding as many different connectors to your presentation as possible will increase audience attention, understanding, and the overall impact of your information.

> **Use as many connectors as possible throughout your presentation**

# USE EXAMPLES and COMPARISONS

· · · · · · · · · · · · · · · · · · · · · · · · · · · · · · · · · ·

Here is a list of examples, comparisons, and analogies that I will use to demonstrate my points:

_____

_____

_____

_____

_____

_____

_____

_____

_____

_____

_____

# PARTICIPATION

It's one thing to just show up and do a bang-up job in your speaking role. It's another thing to play a key role as a participant in the entire event, from preparation through to the finish—to, in effect, act as a host, even if you're not officially hosting.

The following chapters identify ways that you can create an environment that will be conducive to active participation by you, your fellow speakers, and your audience.

**7**

# Secrets of
# Successful Hosting

This chapter unveils secrets that professional speakers and talk show hosts use to create positive engagement with their audiences. Study from the masters, and you can create the same level of engagement with your own audience.

Did you know the conversations that you see on talk shows are not spontaneous? The guest tells the host, in advance, to ask them certain questions so that they can share the stories they have prepared. Is that sneaky? No! It's entertainment.

As a presenter, you are also an entertainer. This assertion may surprise you, but before you discount it, consider the definition of "entertain":

"To hold attention pleasantly," per Dictionary.com.

"To interest somebody," per OxfordDictionary.com.

To change minds or actions, you must hold an audience's attention. If they are not paying attention, they can't be engaged. And if they aren't engaged, you have little chance of success. Whether you are the keynote speaker, the emcee, a panelist, or simply making a sponsor statement, you are "hosting" the audience for the time that you are on deck. There are several tactics that you can apply to give you and your audience the best chance to make a connection.

## Meet Your Audience

Even as a guest presenter, you become the host while you are presenting. So be a good host and arrive early to meet and greet the audience. Get to know a bit about the audience members. This extra effort really pays off when you later show up on stage and are recognized by various audience members, who are thinking or saying things like:

"I just chatted with her at the coffee station and she was really nice."

or

"He said hi to me when I walked in."

Because you took the time to greet them, those audience members now have a connection to you and don't see you as just some anonymous speaker who suddenly appears on the stage.

For example, imagine that you are in Chicago giving a presentation about air quality. Before things get started, you are chatting with guests at the coffee station and one of them says that they grew up in Nashville, Tennessee. It just so happens that you also grew up there.

You can use that information in your opening comments and say:

> "I was just speaking with Norm about 10 minutes ago and he told me that he grew up in my hometown of Nashville and remembers the air being crisp and clean as a child. What do you all remember about the air quality where you grew up?"

This will allow you to immediately connect with the audience. Your small connection with Jeff can extend to the rest of the audience and help people relate to you. When one audience member is participating or being included, everyone feels as if they are, too. And the more people you speak with, the more of these connections you can make. You will hopefully learn some names and get a sense of people whom you might call on as you engage with the audience.

This is also possible in the virtual world. Ask the organizer (if not you) to allow participants to sign on 15 minutes early. As the early birds log on, you are there to say hello and casually converse. As others sign on, they will observe this and begin to feel connected, even if they don't say anything. And you'll have the same opportunities as outlined above at the coffee station.

But what do you do if you encounter a situation where meeting the audience beforehand simply isn't possible? This happened to me recently when I conducted a continuing education course for attorneys through their local bar association. I was not allowed to know who was registered for the course, and there was to be no voice capability for students or ability to sign on early to chat. It seemed like there would be no way for them to participate in the session.

So I had to employ other connection tactics. First, I was able to obtain general information about the audience from the organizer in advance, such as that there were 12 attorneys from large law firms, 7 attorneys from small firms, several sole practitioners, and so on. Now I knew a little bit about who was on the other end of my computer and was able to incorporate that knowledge into my presentation.

But I still wanted to create some sense of participation and interaction between the audience and me. I didn't want it to be just one-way communication. The solution was to use online polling, a feature available in most video meeting platforms. Everyone got involved by responding to the live poll, and then I discussed the group's responses in the seminar. The other feature I used was the software's "Question and

Answer" area. The seminar did not allow for chat, but I encouraged participants not only to ask questions, but to make comments in the Q&A area. This had the effect of creating the sense of engagement I had been looking for.

I was told later that these efforts made a huge difference and helped my seminar stand out, because normally such seminars are just one-sided lectures. There is normally very little interaction or engagement.

## Plant Questions

A fabulous engagement secret of great presenters is to encourage questions from audience members in advance. For example, in the conversation with Norm at the coffee pot, if Norm had asked the presenter whether his company was being sold, an engaging presenter would likely have responded as follows:

> "I'm so excited that you asked that, and I'll bet other people here are wondering the same thing. Would you mind asking me that during the presentation so I can share the answer with everyone?"

> **Recruit a friend or colleague to ask the first question, giving others the courage to be next.**

If you have a friend or colleague in the audience, recruit them to ask a question if no one else does. In cases where you don't know anyone, ask the organizer if they will do this for you. This ensures that *someone* will ask a question, something that doesn't always happen organically. There are times when no one wants to be first and it can be difficult to get that initial question asked. But once the first person raises their hand, others almost always follow.

All this holds true online as well as in person. Even if there is no live, vocal interaction, the same strategy can be used through the chat function. Ask at least one person in advance to enthusiastically interact in the chat section of your online presentation so that others will feel comfortable doing so as well.

## Award Prizes!

There are all kinds of ways to encourage audience participation, in addition to Q&A. One of our favorite methods, with participants of *any* age, is to offer prizes. Several techniques of giving prizes out may be employed.

Reward the first few comments or questions with prizes and say:

> "Thank you so much for being among the first to chime in."

If no one is participating, try this:

"I have a prize for the first person who can tell me . . ."

The opportunity to win something is very powerful. It doesn't seem to matter what the prize is. Think about those cheap T-shirts shot into the crowd at sports arenas. What do you think is more powerful: the desire for that T-shirt or the desire to be the person who won it? If you've seen this activity, you have probably seen someone get tackled for that T-shirt.

## Everyone loves to win a prize!

I'm not suggesting that you give terrible prizes, but I want to make sure you realize that even a candy bar prize will usually elicit the same response as a $5–$10 prize. And unless your company-logoed gift is something that people would really *want*, they would probably rather have a candy bar!

This is easily done online as well. Ask your sponsor if there are some prizes available for the session. If they are not willing to provide any, invest in a few $5 electronic coffee shop gift cards. Utilize them throughout the session to keep attention and participation high.

I needed to do this for the law seminar referenced above. It can be difficult to get the first person to chime in live or in the chat. Sometimes they need a bit of extra encouragement. But once the first person speaks up, others find their courage and follow suit. When no one initially jumped in to comment online during my law seminar, I offered a "coffee on me" (aka a $5 gift card by email). It worked immediately.

## Participate in Your Own Introduction

Find out if the event host will be introducing you and if they intend to say more than just your name and title. Will your biography appear in a printed program or online in the event's digital program? That's where the audience can see every job you've ever held, all the boards you serve on, and so forth.

If you are to be introduced, be prepared for a less-than-optimal intro. People are usually pretty bad at this. More often than not, they read something you sent them verbatim to the audience, as if they are looking at it for the first time (because they likely are!). And if you sent your whole résumé, they are then faced with attempting to find and read the high-lights under pressure.

There are so many problems with this approach. Not only is this awkward for the host, but the frank truth is that no one wants to be read a list of your accomplishments.

So, help everyone out. Provide the emcee with a "recommended introduction" for their convenience. Write out a 30-second introduction that *can* be read verbatim (and bring an extra copy in case the emcee forgets it). List your current position, of course, but don't go much deeper into your work history. Instead, focus on why you are passionate about the subject or group that you are speaking to. This is why the audience came, after all—so tell them what excites you about the topic or what brought you to be interested in it in the first place. Those who want to research your history and résumé can read your full bio online or in the program.

> ## Don't rely on your résumé as your introduction.

Make it a point to meet the person who is introducing you, if you don't already know them. Ask if they have any questions about your bio. This may cue them to look at it if they haven't yet. You can also remind them how to pronounce your name, if necessary. This intentional interaction gives them the same opportunity referenced above regarding unexpected anecdotes. You may tell them something that works perfectly in their introduction:

> "I was just talking to David and he said that he used to spend his summers here as a child and has fond memories of . . ."

By making this effort, you establish a comfort level and rapport between the two of you, which carries over to the audience and sets a new tone. What an improvement over being introduced by someone whom you've never met and who is struggling through a complicated page of words they've never looked at before!

If there is no introduction at all, it's important to introduce yourself and assert your credibility and/or passion about your topic. In an office setting, with a close group of peers who know your role well, this is likely unnecessary.

## Introducing Others

If you are the emcee or moderator, these strategies are useful as well. You don't get to take a backseat because you are "just" moderating. You set the stage for the whole event and keep it moving. It's up to you to create the excitement, set the tone, and keep everything on track.

When it comes to introductions, make an effort to meet the presenter(s), at least by phone, before the day of the event. If you have no choice but to wait until that day, make the most of it. Allow them to participate in their introduction. Find out how to pronounce their name(s) correctly. Ask what excites them about their topic. Make an effort to introduce them as though you know them. This greatly increases the comfort level of the audience, which will in turn make them more *receptive* to the presenter(s).

## Virtual Hosting

For meetings with more than five or six people, let everyone know in advance that you will call roll, both to find out who is on the call and to set volumes. If someone is coming through especially loud or soft, or is located in a noisy area, this is a good time to ask them to make audio adjustments (or possibly change locations). Start by doing it yourself, then call the names of those expected to be there. Do this for non-video conference calls as well.

Ask if anyone else has joined the call whose name you didn't mention. This is especially useful in identifying people who don't have their cameras on or have dialed in without a name. A strategic way to avoid people talking over each other is to say:

"Did anyone with a last name starting with A through K join?"

For smaller meetings where people don't know each other, make sure you introduce attendees personally or give them the opportunity to introduce themselves at the start of the meeting. People perform better when they are comfortable with each other, which affords a greater degree of candor, participation, and mutual interest. Your job as a leader, particularly when people may not know each other, is to make them feel connected so that you can have a productive meeting with open communication. If appropriate, have each team member take 30–60 seconds to talk about what's going on in their lives, both personally and professionally.

## Setting Virtual Expectations

Just as important as setting the meeting agenda is setting meeting guidelines to establish how spontaneous communications and other issues should be handled. What are the rules and expectations of how the team is expected to contribute to the virtual meeting? Make your expectations known in advance by including them in the meeting invite. Here are some ideas for guidelines to include:

- Can everyone speak freely, or will you call on individuals when it's their turn to contribute?

- Specify whether the meeting is video or audio and ask that everyone sign in with video if that is the expectation.

- Should people mute their phones while others are speaking?

- Will everyone enter in silence and then will you call roll, or should they announce themselves when logging on? (Some programs allow the facilitator to be in charge of everyone's mute/unmute, so consider using that functionality if it's available.)

- Advise that you will call on people, or ask them to use the "raise your hand" feature if your software allows it. Establish some way to reduce the awkwardness of everyone trying to speak or ask questions at once.
- If materials are to be reviewed in advance, set that clear expectation.
- Ask that speakers pause often so that others may contribute, if appropriate.

If all this isn't clear from the outset, it can get very cumbersome and uncomfortable for everyone. It's such a disaster when everyone is speaking over each other or trying to ask questions and not being recognized. Tell people the ground rules in advance and everyone—including *you*—will be much happier!

> Set expectations for virtual meetings.

## Virtual Participation

Your job as a facilitator is to create a space of safety for those individuals who may not be comfortable vocalizing in this forum. If there are people in the meeting who are less comfortable speaking up, structure the meeting in a way that gives everyone equal opportunity for their voices to be heard. A round-robin-style discussion is one solution because it gives everyone a set amount of time to share an insight or experience they've had around the meeting topic.

If you notice that someone on the call is trying to contribute but getting overshadowed by more extroverted participants, carve out time for them to speak. If that isn't working, take the time to schedule a one-on-one to get that person's insights on how you can make remote meetings a more inclusive space for them. Even better, create a communal space or document online where people can add their thoughts, insights, and suggestions during and following the meeting.

And just as in live meetings, you can use prizes to encourage participation. Prizes can be snail-mailed to the winners after the meeting, or a coffee shop gift card or a coupon for your services can be emailed following the meeting.

## Rehearsal

If you are the main host of the meeting and have guest speakers, set up a rehearsal with them before the actual meeting. This will enable you to test their audio and visual setups and to assess their ability to use the software necessary for the meeting. Given the knowledge that you have gained in this book, you may also want to make suggestions about improving their setup and so on. After all, since you are the host, everything reflects on you! Even if you are not the main host but rather a speaker on an upcoming virtual meeting, ask the host if they would conduct a rehearsal for the reasons outlined above.

Visit www.distinguishedcomm.com for a sample of virtual meeting expectations.

# PREPARE TO HOST

How will I meet the audience in advance?

Which questions will I plant?

What prizes can I provide?

**Will I be introduced? How can I help?**

_____

_____

**Am I introducing anyone and how can I make that personal?**

_____

_____

**When is live or virtual rehearsal?**

_____

_____

**Who is setting live or virtual expectations?**

_____

# 8

# Owning the Room

**H**ave you ever attended a presentation where the presenter clearly "owned" the room? Where the presenter seemed to exert a masterful control over not only their performance, but over the entire environment and experience for everyone?

Knowing as much as possible about the presentation space and the audience will dramatically increase your chances of being an effective presenter. Many speakers don't take the time to acquire this information and often end up delivering lacklaster presentations. But trust me on this—doing a bit of homework ahead of time is definitely worth it.

## Ask Questions to Better Prepare

When you are invited to give a presentation (whether online or in person), start with asking the requestor the following questions:

- Who is the audience?
- How many people are expected?
- What is the requestor's goal for the presentation?
- What do they believe the audience wants to know?
- How will the audience benefit from the information?
- How much time do they want you to spend in total?
- Will you be introduced? If so, by whom?
- What time will you have access to the room or virtual room?
- What is the attire?

If the presentation is in person, add the following items to your list of questions:

- How is the room set up? Are the sponsors open to changing it for the presentation if necessary?
- What are the audiovisual capabilities?
- Will there be anyone on-site to assist with audiovisual equipment?
- Will there be a microphone? If so, is it fixed or handheld? Do they have a lavaliere (clip-on microphone)?
- Is there a podium or lectern?

- Are you permitted to provide gifts/ materials/prizes to the audience?

Having all that information will dramatically increase your ability to achieve your presentation goals and decrease any anxiety. If you present to a lot of groups outside your organization, consider developing a form for the requestor to fill out, in writing, with answers to your questions.

Take it a step further by calling the requestor after you receive the answers to further explore their expectations. Naturally, if your boss is asking you to make a presentation to your coworkers, you are not going to ask that she first fill out a form! But you can certainly ask some or all the questions above.

If the requestor doesn't have a lot of answers, ask if you can speak to someone in the group to ensure that you will meet their expectations. Perhaps there is a club president or someone you know who will be attending.

It's worth getting these answers so that you can build the most effective engagement. For example, say that you are a real estate development expert and that you often speak about how to find property for commercial development. Imagine that you have been asked to speak to a group called the Real Estate Development Association. Through your investigative process, you find out that this group is looking for something completely different from what you normally speak about.

It turns out, what they are most interested in is how to partner with foreign firms to expand local development. You were recently quoted in an article about partnering with foreign firms, and that is why the Development Association asked you to present.

This knowledge about the audience's desired topic allows you to create an outline and approach tailored to meet their needs and concerns.

## Use a Microphone to Make Sure Nobody Is Left Behind

If more than 25 people are in the room, *always* use a microphone. Everyone says, "I don't need a microphone." The truth is, we don't know how the volume of our own voices register with others. I've had many students in my seminars who didn't realize that they were being way too loud for the room; and I've had other students who spoke way too softly. What they all had in common was that they thought their volume was appropriate.

> **No one wants to say that they can't hear you.**

Louder students in my seminars seem able to lower their volume pretty easily upon request, but staying consistent is always a challenge. The key for them is to present in their regular speaking voice and use a microphone whenever possible. It's a different story for "low talkers." Remember, the volume we hear in our own heads is not the same as what those around us hear.

I'll never forget the first time I saw this in action. It was in one of the very first seminars I taught, and a student named Jill spoke so softly in her first practice to the group that we could barely hear her. Her volume was practically like a whisper. Only a handful of students were in the room, so they weren't using microphones. I told her to try shouting her presentation as loud as she could just to see how loud she could be. Guess what happened? There was no real increase in her volume. She said, "I'm yelling as loud as I can!"

Since then, I've had that happen with quite a few students. In their own heads, it sounds like they are shouting, but to the audience there is little volume to the speaker's voice. This is a "setting" in the brain and can be worked through with a professional voice coach. "Low talkers" are the exception to the guideline about using a microphone if more than 25 people are in the room. Their threshold should be 10 or more people.

Audience members will almost never say that they can't hear you because they don't want to be rude. They will sit through your entire presentation without hearing clearly and never say a word. Even if you say, "Can you hear me OK?," no one will tell you that they can't. But I can tell you from experience that someone is likely struggling to hear you. Remove that obstacle by using a microphone.

To use a microphone properly, hold it about two to four inches from your mouth, depending on the type. It may seem obvious, but too often I see speakers hold the microphone at their side or elsewhere, but nowhere near their mouth! Consider asking someone in the back of the room to commit to letting you know if you are ever difficult to hear.

Consider requesting a mobile microphone that would allow you to leave the front of the room and walk the aisle to better involve everyone—even those in the last row. But what are the options to be interactive when the furniture is stationary? If possible, you can ask staff members to hold microphones on either side of the room to encourage comments and questions and get more participation from the audience.

Online sound is just as important to ensure that you are able to be heard clearly online. If you are participating in a lot of video meetings, it's worth getting a dedicated microphone or an updated device if you don't have one. With some equipment, it can be more effective to use one device for the camera and another for the sound, so test out combinations with a friend and see which presents you in the most effective way, both visually and audibly.

When people are presenting online, their equipment and bandwidth will vary, which means that speed, pauses, clarity of sound, and visuals will also vary. One thing that will improve the experience for everyone is to take a slight pause between sentences. This enables anyone with a slower system to catch up; it also allows for participants to stop you if necessary. Either way, it's always a good idea to ask, every few minutes, if everyone can see and hear you clearly. Unless you ask, the audience may be hesitant to inform you of sound or visual issues.

## Make the Room's Setup Work for *You*

Everyone's personality and style are different. For those of us who like to walk the room to engage more with the audience, a room set up like the first diagram would not work.

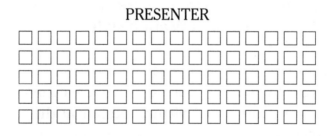

Ask if the room could be set up like this instead:

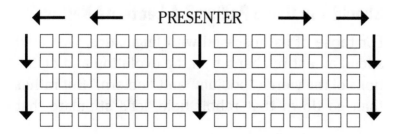

That simple adjustment would give you the ability to engage with more people because you could walk down the center aisle during the presentation. It's not about calling people out in the back who aren't paying attention (after you implement all the tools in this book, you'll be so effective that everyone will pay attention!). It's about creating opportunities to connect with your audience. Connecting is harder when you are far away. Getting closer to more audience members enables you to make better eye contact, give prizes, or show a prop in a more personal way.

If several hundred people are in the room, hopefully there are large screens, at least on either side, so that you are visible to those in the back.

> **Set the room for *your* most effective communication style.**

Find out in advance what the room setup is and strategically plan for *your* most effective communication style. More about virtual setup is at the end of this chapter.

## Should You Use a Podium? A Lectern? Neither?

For those of us obsessed with linguistics, we could spend an entire chapter on the evolution and definitions of the words "podium" and "lectern." But rather than go down that rabbit hole, let's stipulate that both are stands to rest notes, a microphone, and/or water on.

One of the most common questions I receive is about whether or not to use one of these when presenting. There's no easy answer, because it depends on the individual style of the presenter and how they can be most effective. I personally find a big wooden box that hides my entire body from the audience to be a barrier between them and me, so I avoid using one whenever possible. The more modern versions, consisting of just a surface on a pole, are less visually constricting, but they still require me to stay in one place if the microphone is fixed, so I don't like them either.

There's no pressure to make a decision about this right now. I recommend finishing this book, evaluating your own opportunities to be most effective, and then deciding if a podium/lectern/stand fits into your plan. But do make a decision before you get to the room to present. And whatever you do, don't go halfway. By that I mean, don't have the podium there and then stand *next* to it or, what's worse, *lean* on it. Although some people do this in an attempt to look casual, it sends a message to the audience that says, "I don't care enough about this to stand up straight."

## Know the Audiovisual Equipment

Make sure you know what the host will provide regarding audiovisual equipment. Always assume that if something can go wrong, it will. In fact, even if equipment is available, bring your own as backup if possible. Test the equipment, not only when you arrive but ten minutes before your presentation begins, just to be sure.

I have personally experienced electronic challenges more times than I'd like to recall. One reason these challenges happen is that when I show up to the venue, there is some secret to turning on the power to the projector, or to lowering the screen, or to dealing with some other necessary element. And sometimes, there is no one on-site who knows the secrets! Find out in advance if there is anything you may need to know and who will be able to assist if necessary on the day of the presentation.

And even if everything works great at the beginning, the electronic systems can fail halfway through your presentation. This can be an enormous source of stress if you're not prepared, but if you know that you can still make an impact without the electronics, you'll be in great shape.

It is a good idea to invest in and pack your own remote control with your presentation materials at all times. Keep an extra set of fresh batteries, too, just in case. It's distracting not only for you but also for your audience if you have to keep going over to a computer to hit the advance key during a presentation. Use a remote!

## Arrive Early!

Never rush into a presentation at the last minute. Give yourself plenty of time to set things up, test your visuals, place your handouts, and get your head in the right place to present. If you do all those things early and at your own pace, you will be in a much better state of mind to present effectively.

It's important to test the equipment itself, as discussed, but it's also important to view the material on screen. Go to the worst seat in the room and see if the visuals are clear and are not obstructed in some way. If you can't see the visual clearly from there, *change the visual*. You got there early, so now you have the time to do this. And your presentation should be flexible enough that you can change it relatively easily.

Early arrival also means you have time to move the furniture yourself if it's not to your liking. What's more, you now have time to meet and chat with the arriving audience members. This is a great way to reduce anxiety. And someone may unknowingly provide you with an anecdote that allows you to involve the audience in your presentation. (See chapter 6 for more on examples and anecdotes.)

> **Arriving early will greatly increase your ability to succeed—and will reduce anxiety.**

## HOW TO OWN THE ROOM WHEN YOU'RE ONLINE

Owning the virtual room is just as important as owning the physical room, and many of the same tactics apply. Just as stated above, sign on early. Be there smiling and ready when the first people log in. Engage in some conversation if possible before the meeting starts. (See more about this in chapter 7.)

## Technology

When presenting online, especially if logging in to a program that you are not familiar with, ask for a test run. Not every program is the same, and practicing the slide sharing or two-way communication function in advance is important. You don't want to be learning on the spot during your presentation.

## Camera and Lighting

The best place for your device during a video chat is probably different from where you have it for daily work. The ideal position for the camera is a height about equal to the top of your head. It may require balancing your device on some boxes or books, but it's worth it to achieve a professional look to the viewers. Always test your camera before the video call to observe what others will see. Position yourself in a way that makes you centered in the frame. Ensure that there is light in front and above you, not behind you. If you must set up in front of a window, close the shades or shutters and light up your face.

In this screenshot, you can see that the gentleman is looking into the camera and is well lit, and that the camera is positioned correctly. His colleague has the camera below her face and is in front of a window, making her very difficult to see.

## Where to Look

It's OK to look at your audience on screen when *they* are talking, but it's most effective to look directly into the camera when *you* are talking. This makes the audience feel as if you are speaking directly to them. It takes some practice to get used to but is well worth it, as it makes a world of difference in your communication.

Be sure to place yourself an appropriate distance from the camera. The woman below is positioned perfectly, in the center of the frame and looking into the camera. The man is much too close to the camera and is looking at the woman on screen, rather than into the camera.

## Distractions

For some reason, people often feel at liberty to eat, walk around, or do other things while on a video meeting—things they most likely would not do in a live meeting. And even if you might chomp on a granola bar in a live meeting, there wouldn't be a camera-focused close-up on your face. During a video meeting, resist the urge to eat or engage in anything other than the meeting itself.

## Surroundings

If you are presenting virtually, you are in full control of what the setting will be (albeit possibly from the confines of your kitchen or basement). Look around the room. Test the camera. What will others see when they log on?

The scene below is a common yet disturbing one. At least this person is dressed well, as people often are not when working from home. If you are confined to your bedroom for video calls, make sure there is no unmade bed in the background. Better yet, turn the camera around so that there is no bed or dirty laundry in sight at all.

Make yourself an appropriate set for video calls that conveys professionalism. It's amazing what you can do with a nightstand and a houseplant! Here is one of our clients in her makeshift home video set:

Here's what it really looked like:

And here is the same corner of the room, before setting it up for the video:

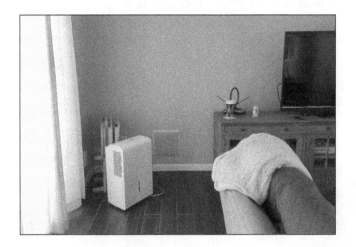

Notice that the background is plain and simple. While it's not meant to look like a professional studio, it looks perfectly appropriate for a home video call. Look around and see where you might set up. Look for locations that will give you not only the privacy you need but also a nondistracting background.

While writing this book, I found myself on an important video call during a stay at a vacation rental. Here is what the room looked like:

To make the room look professional for the call, I had to address the following:

- The room didn't have a desk; just a bed and some chairs.
- One chair had ill-placed artwork for my purposes and the other was in front of a window.
- Clutter was everywhere, both mine and that of the room.
- There was nowhere to put my computer.

Here's what I did to make it look professional:

- I chose the chair at the window but closed the curtains to eliminate back- lighting. (Never have light behind you or you will show up as a silhouette to the viewers.)
- A lamp was placed on the chair in front of me to light my face.
- I removed distractions and unnecessary objects that may be in the frame, such as my shoes, purse, and especially the trash can!
- There was nothing in the room with any height to put my computer on, but I found a chair in the bathroom and set my laptop on that, so the camera was slightly higher than eye level.

- The black chair and gray curtains were really dark and I didn't bring anything colorful to wear. So I grabbed a blanket off the bed and draped it over the chair and found the vase of fake flowers on the nightstand. But the flowers weren't tall enough to be seen. That's why I stacked up a pile of books from the bookcase and placed the flowers on top.

Here is a screenshot of me during the call. Given what I had to start with, I felt it looked clean, clear, and professional. (And no one saw my pajama bottoms or goofy slippers!)

# PLAN TO OWN THE ROOM

· · · · · · · · · · · · · · · · · · · · · · · · · · · · · · · · · · ·

**Ask the host questions in advance:**

- Who is the audience?
- How many people are expected?
- What is the requestor's goal for the presentation?
- What do they believe the audience wants to know?
- How will they benefit from the information?
- How much time do they want you to spend in total?
- Will you be introduced. If so, by whom?
- What time will you have access to the room or virtual room?
- What is the attire?

**Prepare the live or virtual space:**
- Staging
- Furniture
- Lighting
- Test audiovisual

**Be Early!**

**Add the following if the presentation is in person:**

- How is the room set up? Are the sponsors open to changing it for the presentation if necessary?

- What are the audiovisual capabilities?

- Will there be a microphone? If so, is it fixed or handheld? Do they have a lavaliere (clip-on microphone)?

- Is there a podium or lectern?

- Are you permitted to provide gifts/materials/prizes to the audience?

# 9

# Use Notes

There are two opposing schools of thought on using notes: those who love them and those who hate them. I'm a lover not a hater. Here's why: unless you are a professional actor or comedian, a memorized speech will likely sound like a memorized speech. It won't sound authentic and will cause the audience to lose interest.

On top of that, if you forget a line of a memorized dissertation, it may paralyze your ability to move on or may cause you to accidentally skip an entire section. Memorizing a presentation is never recommended.

Using basic notes is liberating. If an audience member comments and interrupts a memorized speech, you'll be thrown off. But if you have simple notes, you can easily get right back on track.

Reading a script is not an option if you want to be effective. Even if you look up periodically to make it appear that you are making eye contact, you will not be successful. Think about times when you've seen a presenter read from notes or from a teleprompter. Doesn't it feel disconnected and disingenuous?

> **Unless you're a professional actor, a script or memorized speech will never sound authentic.**

If you don't know your subject matter, you shouldn't be presenting it. Still, there will almost certainly be a few facts and figures that you want to have in front of you to ensure accuracy. That's why I support having reminder notes, just not a script. It doesn't matter if your notes are on a piece of paper or on note cards.

Effective notes will have a font size large enough for you to see at a glance. No line should be more than a few words, except your opening and closing lines, which I do recommend writing down verbatim.

Let's take another look at Bob's Kids, the slide example used in the chapter 5, the visual aids chapter, pictured again below. What might the presenter's notes look like, based on the information provided? Remember that we narrowed down the words for the slide to simply:

- Success
- Empowerment
- Transformation

Although you shouldn't have more than those words on your actual slide, you can certainly give yourself a few more reminders in your personal notes. Below I have underlined what I feel would make good reminders for notes. You may look at the same slide and underline slightly different words as reminders. Let's focus on what presentation notes should look like.

---

### Bob's Kids

- Through Bob's Kids, at-risk young people can **succeed** with the guidance of a **volunteer mentor** who has chosen to make a **positive impact** on a young person's life.
- Bob's Kids aims to empower youth to fulfill their potential through mentoring and **life skills** development.
- We are a model for what mentoring relationships can be in our community.
- Bob's Kids connects youth ages 7–17 with adult mentors to help kids reach their greatest possible potential. We have a curriculum that focuses on **social and emotional learning**. The curriculum involves programs through which youth acquire and apply knowledge, attitudes, and skills with the support of their mentors.
- Through Bob's Kids, volunteer mentors have transformed the lives of **9,600 youth** through the development of social, emotional, and academic skills with the help of committed volunteers and **community support**.

EXHIBIT O

---

Each main point will require one or more pieces of supporting information, depending on the complexity of the main point. Whatever number of supporting points you choose, your notes should be no more complicated than Exhibit P.

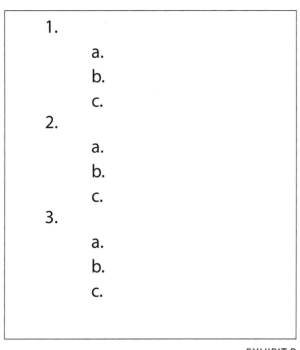

EXHIBIT P

Exhibit Q shows what your basic notes should look like before you add in accompanying emotional connectors. You'll notice it features simple reminders to keep the speaker on track. If you understand your material, you should need only a quick reference to remind you of what to address.

Also included are reminders about your Entrance and your Exit. Take a look.

I'd like to tell you about a homeless boy named Cooper. Tell story.

1. **Success**
   a. Mentoring
   b. Positive impact
   c. Ages 7-17
2. **Empowerment**
   a. Teach life skills
   b. Social/emotional learning
3. **Transformation**
   a. 9,600
   b. Community

Cooper . . . now mentors. Will you join him?

EXHIBIT Q

## Add the Connectors

Once you are practiced at getting your presentation into three categories and identifying which emotional connectors you want to use, you are ready to take your notes to the next level. List all the ways that you will connect with the audience throughout the engagement.

Below is a clue about how to set up your notes to remind you to use the emotional connectors that trigger the senses. If you've followed the steps in this book, your work is already done because you have listed the tools that you will use on the Impact Planner worksheet on page 66.

Now you just transfer those reminders about each slide, visual aid, demonstration, quote, question, example, comparison, and so on to your notes. The best presentations will have an emotional connector listed on every line. But it takes time to get to that level so don't pressure yourself. Start by ensuring that you have at least one connector for each main point. Over time, work to incorporate as many as possible.

In the presentation to prospective mentors about Bob's Kids, the presenter Enters with a story about Cooper (see chapter 2). He could show a photo when he talks about the success of the program. He might share a famous quote about empowerment in section 2. When discussing transformation, he might compare Cooper to a caterpillar changing into a butterfly. For his Exit, he finishes the story about Cooper and asks the audience to mentor.

| KEYWORDS | EMOTIONAL CONNECTORS |
|---|---|
| I'd like to tell you about a homeless boy named Cooper . . . | Story |
| | |
| **1. Success** | Photo |
| Mentoring | |
| Positive impact | |
| Ages 7–17 | |
| | |
| **2. Empowerment** | Empowerment Quote |
| Teach life skills | |
| Social/emotional learning | |
| | |
| **3. Transformation** | Caterpillar/Butterfly Analogy |
| a. 9,600 | |
| b. Community | |
| | |
| Cooper . . . now mentors. Will you join him? | Story/Question |

EXHIBIT R

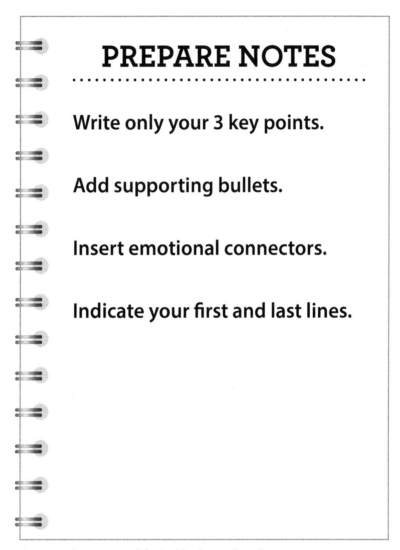

# PREPARE NOTES

Write only your 3 key points.

Add supporting bullets.

Insert emotional connectors.

Indicate your first and last lines.

*On our website, you will find a blank template that you can print and use any time that you are planning a presentation. www.distiguishedcomm.com.*

# Choosing a Coach

After every speech, toast, or presentation, the three most common words of feedback are: "You were great."

What do those words mean? As a speaker, you want to believe those words. As listeners, we may have thought the speech was terrible, yet we still tell the presenter they were "great." Why do we do this?

It happens because we are uncomfortable giving and receiving constructive feedback, not just in the context of public speaking but in life in general. It's a bit like asking people "How are you?" and not really wanting to know the true answer. Our expectation is that the response will be "Good." Anything more detailed is likely to be met with discomfort.

Reading this book and adapting its lessons into your communication is an excellent start to becoming a more effective presenter and communicator. However, to truly take your skills to the next level, I recommend working with a professional presentation coach. A coach not only will give you honest, constructive feedback but will teach you how to make the most of that feedback.

> ## No one wants to hear a long list of things they are doing wrong.

The best coaching involves one-on-one individualized tutoring. Coaches will find the areas where you already excel, assess your potential, and work with you to maximize your best skills. Every presenter has their own personality and style, and it's up to the coach to focus on bringing out your strengths and finding what is magic about *you*.

Don't hesitate to meet with several coaches to see who you feel most comfortable with and whose approach you think best fits your needs. A good coach should be more than willing to do that.

Word to the wise: Be careful about attending community practice groups. Some are great, but unless there is a professional coach in charge of giving feedback, they can be very damaging. The group could be made up of really bad speakers giving their poorly conceived personal opinions. A professional coach in charge of a group will provide a trained opinion and specific tools for each participant to grow and improve.

Should you join a practice group, be aware of the type of feedback you will receive. Ask yourself these questions:

- Are there professional communication coaches giving constructive feedback?
- Have you seen the people offering the feedback give an effectivepresentation ?
- Do you agree with their presentation style enough to trust their feedback?

If your answer to all these questions is yes, then you may have found a valuable practice group. If your answer is no, the group has the potential to deliver more harm than good.

A class should focus on live practice and feedback. If you plan to take a class with others, find out how much of the class time will be devoted to live practice and feedback. If it's all about *telling* you what to do, you can read the same in this book.

When it comes to learning, at Distinguished Communications we work on "feed-*forward*" rather than feed*back*. We focus on what the speaker does *well* and build from there, looking ahead to the next opportunity. Public speaking can be nerve racking enough: no one needs to hear a long list of things that they are doing wrong. Feel free to give me a call to see if I or someone on my team is a good fit for you. If we are not a good fit, we can always refer you to a colleague who may be just who you are looking for.

# FEEDBACK and COACHING

If joining a practice group, choose carefully.

Avoid one-size-fits-all coaching.

Look for feedback based on your strengths.

Seek out coaching based on live practice, not lecture.

# Final Thoughts

Don't pressure yourself to do everything in this book immediately. Why not choose one or two things to incorporate into your next communication exchange and see if you notice a difference in the response? If you do, keep doing those things and then add another and another.

It may seem like a lot of work, but I can promise you this: effective presenters aren't just "winging it." They are putting in the advance work to make it *look* like they are winging it. So, if you want to be effective and get results, I encourage you to put in the work.

It's not easy to change your presentation style when you've been doing it a certain way for a long time. But once you get into the habit of planning your communication with the Enter, Enlighten, and Exit model, you will find it useful in countless situations. As an example, let's take a look at the common messaging task of leaving a voicemail. Before leaving your next voicemail, take a moment to ask yourself:

- How will I grab their attention? (Enter)
- What do they need to know from this voice-mail that will help them? (Enlighten)
- Which words will I say last? (Exit)

Do the same thing as you construct content-driven emails. Think this way before walking into the boss's office to ask for something you want. Use this model to propose your destination choice for the next family vacation. These situations just take a moment or two of thought.

Thank you for giving the EEE method a chance. I hope it makes good sense to you and that you can apply these techniques in a variety of ways to improve your communications professionally and personally. Let me know how it goes. I love to hear about my students' and readers' communication experiences—what's working and what's not. Please send me a note through my website: www.distinguishedcomm.com.

As we go our separate ways for now, I'll leave you with a quote from my dear friend, Mark Twain, who said:

"It usually takes me more than three weeks to prepare a good impromptu speech."

I'm not suggesting that you spend weeks to plan every communication, but effective presentations do take work. Mark Twain's speeches were more than good or great. They were goal oriented and effective, and they inspired his audiences to feel. And now you and your speeches can do the same.

# Worksheets

# Goal-Setting Planner

## What do I hope to achieve with this presentation?

## Who is my audience? What is in it for them (WIIFT)?

# ENTER-ENLIGHTEN-EXIT

. . . . . . . . . . . . . . . . . . . . . . . . . . . . . . . . . . . . . . . . . .

**ENTER**

Start with a story, quote, catchy one-liner, question, demonstration—anything to grab attention—but not a topic sentence!

**ENLIGHTEN**

- Group all ideas into 3 main categories.
- Give each category a name.
- Create notes in outline form.
- Devise a plan to stay on time.

**EXIT**

End with a story, quote, catchy one-liner, question, demonstration—anything that says "I'm done." But don't end with a summary!

*A blank template is available for your use at www.distinguishedcomm.com.*

# Managing Fear

- Focus on the goal.

- Get there or sign on early.

- Use notes.

- Avoid caffeine and ice.

- Breathe between thoughts.

- Ask questions to create pauses.

- Stand up straight, shoulders back, feet hip-width apart.

- Prep with deep breathing exercise.

# IMPACT PLANNER

How do I want my audience to *feel* as a result of this presentation?

What thoughts or behaviors am I trying to solidify or change?

Which sensory tool(s) will I use to reinforce each data point? (Feelings and Sight, Smell, Taste, Sound, Touch)

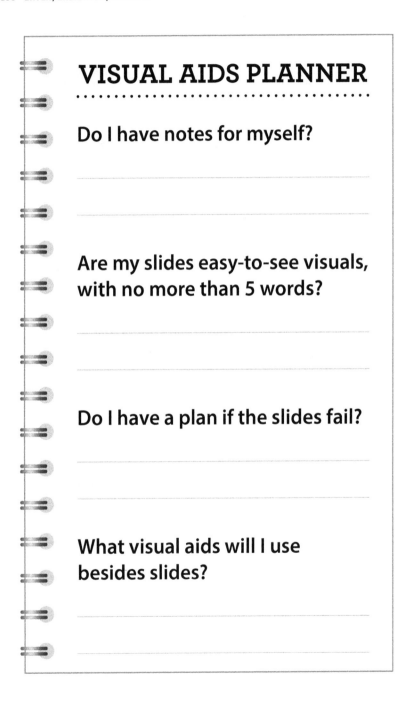

# VISUAL AIDS PLANNER

Do I have notes for myself?

Are my slides easy-to-see visuals, with no more than 5 words?

Do I have a plan if the slides fail?

What visual aids will I use besides slides?

# USE EXAMPLES and COMPARISONS

· · · · · · · · · · · · · · · · · · · · · · · · · · · · · · · ·

**Here is a list of examples, comparisons, and analogies that I will use to demonstrate my points:**

# PREPARE TO HOST

How will I meet the audience in advance?

Which questions will I plant?

What prizes can I provide?

Will I be introduced? How can I help?

Am I introducing anyone and how can I make that personal?

When is live or virtual rehearsal?

Who is setting live or virtual expectations?

# PLAN TO OWN THE ROOM

**Ask the host questions in advance:**

- Who is the audience?
- How many people are expected?
- What is the requestor's goal for the presentation?
- What do they believe the audience wants to know?
- How will they benefit from the information?
- How much time do they want you to spend in total?
- Will you be introduced. If so, by whom?
- What time will you have access to the room or virtual room?
- What is the attire?

**Prepare the live or virtual space:**
- Staging
- Furniture
- Lighting
- Test audiovisual

**Be Early!**

**Add the following if the presentation is in person:**

- How is the room set up? Are the sponsors open to changing it for the presentation if necessary?

- What are the audiovisual capabilities?

- Will there be a microphone? If so, is it fixed or handheld? Do they have a lavaliere (clip-on microphone)?

- Is there a podium or lectern?

- Are you permitted to provide gifts/materials/prizes to the audience?

# PREPARE NOTES

Write only your 3 key points.

Add supporting bullets.

Insert emotional connectors.

Indicate your first and last lines.

*On our website, you will find a blank template that you can print and use any time that you are planning a presentation. www.distiguishedcomm.com.*

# FEEDBACK
## and COOACHING

If joining a practice group, choose carefully.

Avoid one-size-fits-all coaching.

Look for feedback based on your strengths.

Seek out coaching based on live practice, not lecture.

# Acknowledgments

To my family and friends who carefully read manuscript drafts along the way and gave me thoughtful input, thank you: Jeff, Mom, Dad, Dan, David, Jill, and Mary.

To my editor, Kent Sorsky, without whom these pages may not have made any sense, even to me.

To the artists and models who gave their skills and/or selves to these pages, thank you: Lena, Mary, Theron, Juili, Amit, and Davidson Belluso.

To my professional mentors-turned-dear-friends, who modeled stellar communication that carried me through my challenging and rewarding career, thank you: Carol Clements, Danny Murphy, and Penny Pfaelzer.

To my first-ever coach, Christine Muldoon, who set the stage for me to dedicate myself to the pursuit of improving communication for myself and others.

To my parents, who pushed me to have every possible experience, and supported me, even if they didn't agree with my choices—all of which built who I am today—thank you.

To my husband Jeff, whose love and encouragement allowed me to dedicate so much time, energy, and thought to these pages: thank you, my love.

While a piece of my soul is now on every page, it filled and energized me enormously as I crafted each word.

# About the Author

 Deborah Ostreicher spent over 25 years in leadership positions around the globe, including as marketing director for a multinational, hi-tech company in central Europe, as events manager for Prince Charles in the United Kingdom, and as vice president of Phoenix Sky Harbor International Airport.

Ostreicher has spent a lifetime in front of audiences, first as a dancer and musician, then as an award-winning actress, and later as an accomplished television and radio show host. Her performance skills serve her well as an expert speaker and communication coach.

Her undergraduate degree in liberal arts, cum laude, is from the University of Maryland, College Park; her MBA is from the American University, Washington, DC; and her certificate in leadership communication is from Harvard University.

She is now president of Distinguished Communications, an international firm that dramatically improves communication for individuals, for teams, and for entire organizations. She has been quoted in numerous articles on communication, including in Huff Post and Thrive Global, and is coauthor of the book *The Art of Effective Communication*, by Lovely Silks Press.

Ostreicher is based in Phoenix, Arizona, but travels the world to spread the word about the importance of effective communication and how to achieve it.

CPSIA information can be obtained
at www.ICGtesting.com
Printed in the USA
BVHW040556200921
617079BV00002B/12